Springer Series

FOCUS ON MEN

James Hennessy, Ph.D., Series Editor

Focus on Men provides a wide range of books on the major psychological, medical, and social issues confronting men today.

VOLUME 1
CIRCUMCISION: An American Health Fallacy
Edward Wallerstein

VOLUME 2
MEN IN THEIR FORTIES: The Transition to Middle Age
Lois M. Tamir, Ph.D.

Lois M. Tamir, Ph.D., is a developmental psychologist who has done research in the areas of life-span changes, the family life cycle, old age, middle age, and interpersonal communication. She received her B.A. in sociology(*summa cum laude,* 1974) from the State University of New York at Stony Brook, and her Ph.D. in psychology (1980) from the University of Michigan. For two years she worked as a research fellow at the Institute for Social Research for the University of Michigan. Currently, Dr. Tamir is continuing to teach, research, and write as a faculty member of the Psychology Division of the University of Texas Health Science Center. She also maintains an adjunct assistant professorship at the University of Texas at Dallas' Department of Psychology and Human Development.

Men in Their Forties

The Transition to Middle Age

Lois M. Tamir, Ph.D.

Springer Publishing Company
New York

For my parents

Springer Publishing Company, Inc.
200 Park Avenue South
New York, New York 10003

82 83 84 85 86 / 10 9 8 7 6 5 4 3 2 1

Library of Congress Cataloging in Publication Data

Tamir, Lois M.
    Men in their forties.

    (Springer series, focus on men ; 2)
    Bibliography: p.
    Includes index.
    1. Middle-aged men—United States.
2. Fathers—United States.   3. Life cycle,
Human.   I. Title.   II. Series.   [DNLM:
1. Life style—In middle age.   2. Men—
Psychology.   3. Middle age—Psychology.
W1 SP685K v. 2 / BF 724.6 T158m]
HQ1090.3.T35   305.2'4   81-14328
ISBN 0-8261-3630-3   AACR2
ISBN 0-8261-3631-1 (pbk.)
ISSN 0277-3422

Printed in the United States of America

Contents

Foreword by Joseph Veroff, Ph.D.   *vii*
Preface and Acknowledgments   *ix*

1. **The Meaning of Middle Age**   1

   Middle-Aged Men: A Special Population   *1*
   Quality of Life Experience and the Middle-Aged Man   *4*
   Work and the Middle-Aged Man   *12*
   Family and the Middle-Aged Man   *15*
   Social Relationships and the Middle-Aged Man   *19*
   A Plan for the Study of Middle-Aged Men   *20*

2. **A Method for the Study of Middle-Aged Men**   22

   The Survey   *22*
   The Study Sample   *24*
   Analysis Strategy   *27*
   The Structure of Results   *35*

3. **Quality of Life Experience at Middle Age**   37

   Measures of Quality of Life Experience   *37*
   Results: Age Differences in Quality of Life Experience   *42*
   Results: Age Interactions in Measures of Well-Being   *64*
   Summary of Results   *67*

4. **Work at Middle Age**   69

Measures of Work   *69*
Results: Age Differences   *72*
Results: Age Interactions in Measures of Work   *82*
Results: Age Interactions between Work and Well-Being   *90*
Summary of Results   *93*

5. **Family at Middle Age**   96

Measures of Family Life   *96*
Results: Age Differences   *97*
Results: Age Interactions in Measures of Family Life   *100*
Results: Age Interactions between Family and Well-Being   *102*
Summary of Results   *104*

6. **Social Relationships at Middle Age**   106

Measures of Social Relationships   *106*
Results: Age Differences   *108*
Results: Age Interactions in Measures of Social Relationships   *110*
*Results: Age Interactions between Social Relationships
    and Well-Being*   *110*
Summary of Results   *114*

7. **Men at Middle Age: The Total Picture**   117

The Exploratory Method   *118*
*Quality of Life at Middle Age: Internal State and External
    Influences*   *119*
Suggestions for Future Research   *124*

Appendixes   *127*
References   *144*
Index   *149*

Foreword

Very few research reports in the social sciences inspire among their readers a sense that they are on the trail of a discovery. Many investigate social problems for which solutions are needed; many lay out and explore a systematic model of possible psychological determinants of such problems; many ingeniously analyze a complex array of the determinants; and a few even sample a truly representative group of people. Only a handful, however, do all of these, while making readers excited about knowing the outcome of the undertaking. Dr. Tamir's exploration of midlife concerns of American men in the 1970s is such a venture. From her beginning formulation of the study to its conclusion, readers feel in total alliance with the author; so much so that they treat the complex but tightly woven results as they would the denouement of a good mystery story.

Dr. Tamir did find men at midlife to be different from both younger and older men in clearcut ways, especially when she imposed the critical control of educational level in her analyses. The author, nurtured first as a sociologist and then as a life-span developmental psychologist, rediscovered the importance of social status as a critical modifier of developmental transitions. That discovery enriches her work and puts the study of men's life-span issues where it belongs—smack in the middle of their ongoing social lives. Too often developmental psychologists make life-span processes too abstract by assuming that, while people age within specific social historical contexts, life-span principles should transcend these contexts. This assumption normally makes academic researchers avoid asking about the social texture of people's lives and leads them to probe only about universal, general changes in human development. This book averts such a pitfall; instead, it capitalizes on how the particular jobs that men have, the particular people and groups they attend to in their everyday lives shape considerably different reactions for men of different social statuses in American society. We are used to that approach in journalistic accounts, but too often yearn for it in carefully analyzed reports of research. Dr. Tamir presents data that show 40- to 49-year-old men react to being that age in modes that are adaptive to their place in the social structure. These differing reactions, she persuasively argues, represent a common developmental transition. Had she looked at the results without taking account of these different social contexts, her findings would be minimal and confusing.

Not all of the sense of discovery coming from this exciting book hinges on the scientific interests of the readers. Those of us at Michigan who were privileged to read or hear about this study before its publication were personally intrigued with the study, either because we ourselves were men who were approaching, experiencing, or just beyond the midlife period, or because we were related to men who were experiencing these transitions. We were intrigued, as we were with Sheehy's *Passages* or with Levinson's *The Seasons of a Man's Life*, because of our very human desire to code and match our own experiences against data presented from other people's lives. We wanted to gain those special insights that occur when social comparisons make vivid some important feelings or thoughts that have been considered only subliminally or casually.

Dr. Tamir avoids being glib. By sensitively threading a complex set of findings, she presents clearly reasoned but imaginative integrations. Unlike results presented in Sheehy's or Levinson's work, her data are based on a national representative sample; consequently, readers looking for either personal social comparisons or scientific generalizations are on safer grounds in this volume.

Here then is one of the most provocative and integrated research reports to come from Michigan's Survey Research Center in a long time. Written in flowing prose and yet couched in sophisticated analyses and presentations, it is one of those rare number-based research studies that satisfy readers' scientific questions but force them to think beyond graphs, percentages, and statistical significance to the meaning, in this case, of men's experiences through the life cycle.

Joseph Veroff, Ph.D.

Preface and Acknowledgments

Middle age today represents a highly ambiguous set of circumstances. The middle-aged adult is typically at the peak of earning power and status, yet also the butt of jokes and snickers about the "midlife crisis." Some adults expect it to be a period of depression and experience it as such, while others seem to sail through this period with minimal distress. There certainly are enough popular books and articles that deal with the topic of middle age, yet few document their midlife theories with more than anecdotal excerpts or general impressions of interview materials. Large, representative samples of middle-aged adults have not been studied to date.

As a researcher in the field of life-span developmental psychology, I was pleased to find that national data were in fact available and impatiently awaiting analysis, especially in light of popular speculations concerning middle age. A body of national survey data collected in 1976 by the Institute for Social Research at the University of Michigan, entitled "A Study of Modern Living," appeared to contain not only a large sample of adults of all ages, but also an abundance of information on nearly all aspects of lifestyle, work, family, and the mental health of its respondents. I am grateful to Joseph Veroff and Elizabeth Douvan, who headed this project, for their encouragement while I participated in the research group that worked with this marvelous data.

My original approach to the "Study of Modern Living" data was not, however, in an effort to study middle age, but to analyze from a developmental perspective age and life-stage trends throughout the life course. Yet, most of my analyses, be they of family life stage, use of mental-health services, social supports, or other related topics, would reveal the middle-aged group as atypical; hence, I came to the conclusion that an intensive analysis of middle age was certainly in order. This book represents that effort.

The pages that follow describe those characteristics unique to the period of middle age, in particular, the transition to middle age among men of differing class backgrounds. Many results are surprising, while others seem to complement one's common sense. This exploratory effort represents the fundamentals of middle age and will raise issues for future researchers of adulthood change and development. We will need to know more of the long-term outcomes of middle-age phenomena, for old age may confront the individual with even greater developmental challenges. We also will need to know if future cohorts in our society will experience a similar transition when they become middle aged and if they will fare better or worse than their fathers of past generations. This book provides to its readers the basic contours of the period called middle age. I hope that it will serve as an impetus to others to further investigate these contours and provide embellishments, background, and color in an exploration of the middle-age transition and its place in the puzzle of life-span development.

The encouragement, support, and concrete assistance of many individuals helped to make this research project a thoroughly enjoyable and fruitful experience from initial conception to final product.

First and foremost, I owe my thanks to Joseph Veroff and Elizabeth Douvan, who head The Family and Sex Roles Program at The University of Michigan's Institute for Social Research. They most generously shared with me and my colleagues the national survey data from which this research was derived. Their conceptual insights, scholarly attention, and abundant support were invaluable; their work was inspirational. Richard Kulka, James House, and Martin Hoffman also deserve special thanks for the sharing of their methodological experience and expertise and for the clarity of their critical commentaries at all stages of this work.

I also am indebted greatly to a number of persons who have offered their input and expertise at key points in this project. Most notably, David Klingel, Lynn Kahle, and Steven Dubnoff provided me with statistical information essential to the analyses. The editorial assistance of Barbara Watkins of Springer Publishing has been immensely helpful, too. My colleagues within the Family and Sex Roles Program served to establish collectively an intellectually stimulating and socially rewarding atmosphere in which to work. Through this program, my work was supported by a research training grant (MH-14618) from the National Institute of Mental Health.

Lastly, I would like to express my gratitude to my husband, Ron Tamir, whose enthusiasm and support have provided me with assistance throughout.

1

The Meaning of Middle Age

Middle-Aged Men:
A Special Population

Development throughout the life span encompasses a process of continual change and reorganization, both within the individual and between individuals and their social world. This process is well documented in studies of infants, children, and adolescents. There is, however, a conspicuous lack of knowledge about adult developmental change. In light of the increasing longevity of adults born in the twentieth century, the phase of life called adulthood merits further investigation, for the years from early adulthood to old age are far from uniform in terms of external activity and internal life. Middle-aged people constitute a special population among adults because they are no longer young, yet not truly old.

Middle-aged adults constitute the most influential segment of the adult population. They are the most powerful and wealthy age group in the United States, a fact recognized by young, old, and middle-aged alike (Cameron, 1970). They contribute the most toward the maintenance of the structure of society and its normative demands, and by middle age the adult becomes most aware of this awesome responsibility (Neugarten, 1968b, 1973). Schaie (1977–1978) labels this stage of development the "responsible stage," and states that, for many, societal systems, instead of simple individualized units, become the concern of the adult. The big picture has come into focus for the adult at middle age.

There recently has been a growing interest in this group of adults. Just at a time of life when peak performance is expected, increasing recognition of the stresses experienced by the middle-aged adult are coming to light. The term "midlife crisis" in turn has become a commonly used and accepted phrase. The popular literature attests to this point: there is a proliferation of handbooks for dealing with midlife woes (for example, Fried, 1976; Gould, 1978; LeShan, 1973; Mayer, 1978; Sheehy, 1974). However, academic research concerning this topic is sparse. Virtually no survey research project has addressed this developmental issue, although several more clinically derived accounts appear to confirm the idea that middle-aged adults confront a unique set of problems. It is during this period that adults take stock, assess their careers, launch their children, deal with imperfectly functioning bodies, and come to terms with mortality.

Who Is Middle Aged?

As generally conceived, the period called middle age lacks a well-defined boundary (Borland, 1978; Kerckhoff, 1976). It can range anywhere from 30 to 60 years of age. Additionally, Neugarten & Datan (1974) assert that biological and social cues are better indicators of developmental change than age alone. Yet careful reading of the literature on adult development nearly always pinpoints the site of midlife changes as during the 40s decade of life. For example, Jung (1933) describes the onset of middle age, "the afternoon of life," as occurring by the age of 40. Soddy (1967), in a book that describes the conclusions of an international and interdisciplinary conference about middle age, describes this period of life as beginning at about age 40 and signifying the end of a "latency" period of adulthood while initiating a period of "alteration of identity and relearning" (p. 347). Similarly, Fried (1976) views the 40s decade as analogous to a second adolescence, and Vaillant (1977) asserts that at about age 40 the male adult becomes an "explorer" of the "world within" (p. 220). Levinson (1978), too, in his intensive biographical analysis of 40 middle-aged men, finds that prior to about age 40 the man experiences little self-reflection, as he strives to achieve his career goals, receive approval from others, and become an independent adult. At about age 40, attitudes change, toward others and toward oneself, through a process of self-appraisal.

In addition, other studies have shown that both young and old adults view the approximate age of 40 as signifying middle age (Drevenstedt, 1976; Jackson, 1974). Identification by others as one who is middle aged certainly conveys a message of age-related status to adults who have just turned 40, whether they feel middle aged or not.

The Transition

For these reasons, the *transition* to middle age, for the purposes of the present review of the literature and following research design, is defined as occurring between ages 40 and 49. This definition is based on the previous adult life-span literature, which explores, discusses, or sometimes only hints at changes in adult development that occur within this period of time. Because this period is identified as a time encompassing a state of transition, developmental theory also leads the analyst to assume that it is a time of potential stress, as new beginnings are sought and old habits, behaviors, dreams, and goals are reconsidered carefully. Periods of transition are characterized by asynchronies on many levels of activity and development: biological, psychological, sociological, and outer-physical (Riegel, 1972, 1975). The contradictions embodied within this state of asynchrony must be reconciled, difficult though the process may be; for only then can the individual reach a new developmental level. More simply, Brim (1976) identifies the individual in transit as suffering temporary ''growing pains.'' Issues in conflict are brought to light, and solutions are attempted. These tensions are reflected in the inner and outer world of the adults: in the quality of their life experience, their work behavior, their family life, and their social relationships.

Men versus Women

Prior to a discussion of the quality of life, work, family, and social relationships of the middle-aged adult, it should be noted that only the male, and not the female, in middle age will be described and analyzed in the following research design. Research on middle age remains sparse, yet there is more scholarly work available concerning the midlife male than female, and this lends itself to more conclusive (though nonetheless tenuous) descriptions of the male developmental pattern.

More importantly, however, the life course of men and women during adulthood proceeds along different tracks (Maas & Kuypers, 1974). They view the timing of their lifelines from differing vantage points. Women measure personal growth and aging by the sequence of the family cycle, men by events in the world of work. Hence, the process of self-appraisal for women is stimulated by the launching of the children, for men by the stage of occupational achievement (Thurnher, 1974). Whereas middle-aged males may decide to deemphasize the importance of their work, the middle-aged female may be discovering unrealized career potential (Mayer, 1969). Overall, Lowenthal, Thurnher, et al. (1975) report that differences between men and women during adulthood often are greater than differences between age groups.

Predictors of life satisfaction, in turn, differ for middle-aged men and women. One study, for example, found that health and friendship predict life satisfaction for men, but not for women; and that, while men are more satisfied with work, women are more satisfied with family and friends (Mancini, 1978). Additionally, age may be a more pivotal indicator of personal change for men than women. Breytspraak (1974) found that, whereas age is an important predictor of self-concept for men, it has no significance for women in the domain of self-perception.

Clearly, men and women during middle age (as well as throughout the entire life span) comprise two very different subject populations. It also may be that men in their 40s constitute a more stressed group of adults than do women. If the transition to middle age does involve a period of self-assessment and altered relationships with the outside world, it is most likely a more poignant experience for the man than for the woman. This is because coming to terms with emotions may be a new experience for the man. It is women, not men, who have been more emotionally attuned to others and themselves throughout their entire lives (Lowenthal & Robinson, 1976). It is not surprising, therefore, that Meile (1969) reports that at middle age the rate of psychiatric treatment of men first begins to exceed that of women.

For these reasons it seems unwise to group men and women together when undertaking an analysis of the transition to middle age, lest the unique issues salient to men and women in the areas of quality of life experience, work, family, and social relationships run the risk of remaining undiscovered.

Quality of Life Experience and the Middle-Aged Man

A Crisis?

Personality and survey research over the years has monitored the quality of life of adults at different ages. Longitudinal researchers also have attempted to measure how content their long-term subjects are at different points during their lives. Results have been inconsistent. Some studies indicate minimal age differences in life satisfaction (Andrews & Withey, 1976; Neugarten, 1973). Others indicate increased life satisfaction with increased age, or a peak immediately prior to old age (Bourque & Back 1969; Campbell et al., 1976; Clausen, 1972, 1976). Interpreting these types of results, however, presents a formidable task. What constitutes happiness may be different from one age to the next (Cutler, 1979). This point is illustrated best in the survey research results of Campbell et al. (1976), who found an increase in life satisfaction with age but a decrease in happiness. They explain this puzzling result by differentiating satisfaction and happiness. Satisfaction occurs when the individual becomes better accommodated to the environment. This is more likely to occur with increasing age and experience. The young are happy but also can afford to be dissatisfied, since they are hopeful about the improvements that the future will offer. Old age reveals to the adult the more sobering indications of realistic future growth; he must become more satisfied with the present, for it will not be altered greatly. Midway between the young and old falls the transitional middle-aged group, however, a group that Campbell et al. report falls *below* the means of all others in both happiness and satisfaction.

Campbell et al.'s findings are far from isolated results. An upsurge of mental-health problems are reported at about the age of 40, and the anxiety symptoms displayed come in many forms (Soddy, 1967). Jung (1933) discussed many years earlier a rise in the frequency of cases of mental depression among men around their fortieth year. Lowenthal & Chiriboga (1972), in their interviews with middle-aged men, found that the men admitted to experiencing more low points in their lives around the ages of 39 to 46 (the interviews were four years later), a time of increased incidence of nervous breakdowns, physical illness, financial crises, and marital problems. Other researchers have noted a marked increase in neurotic and functional disorders, as well as psychiatric treatment, among men in their 40s (Meile, 1969; Soddy, 1967). Less drastic are the results reported by Frenkel-Brunswik (1968) in a European study of approximately 400 biographies undertaken close to 50 years ago. She reports that men aged 45 to 48 years take more trips and change residence most often, indicative of a period of unrest. These men were inclined to daydream, retrospect, and display transitory interests, unlike men older or younger than themselves. Clearly, something unique seems to occur to a man as he becomes middle aged, for, time and again, studies that range over the entire life span of the individual uncover an atypical statistic, a slump in a curve, or a qualitative shift among their middle-aged subjects, although more often than not this group originally was not meant to be the focus of attention. Clearly, then, this group merits investigation in its own right, and only by evaluating the individual by means of multiple mental-health criteria can a truly accurate picture emerge (Veroff, Feld, et al., 1962).

The Problems: Concrete and Covert

The middle-aged man often confronts very concrete emotional losses: children leave home, parents die, and multiple options for the future diminish (Borland, 1978). In fact, several writers and researchers point to the limitations on one's future as the pivotal middle age issue. Lowenthal, Thurnher, et al. (1975) report that of all the age groups they interviewed, the middle-aged men perceived the bleakest future. They concluded that the strains and boredom of middle age severely threaten the mental health of this group of men. Bardwick (1978) views this predicament from a different angle. She asserts that middle age represents a time in life unadorned by special events that belong solely to the middle aged adult. No longer are there celebrations of one's own graduation, marriage or reproduction, or even of the purchase of one's first home. At the same time, the middle-aged man must view from the sidelines both the pleasures and the challenging struggles that enrich the lives of the young, who may be perceived as a personal threat to the "over-the-hill" middle-aged person in a youth-oriented society (Bard-wick, 1978; Fried, 1976; Levinson, 1978; Lowenthal, Thurnher, et al., 1975).

An important issue that confronts the middle-aged man concerns finan-cial planning for the future. Preoccupation with the material security of his family and its future characterizes the middle-aged men interviewed by Lowenthal, Thurnher, et al. (1975). On a broader level, the status of middle age represents the peak of power and the brunt of decision making and responsibility for others. Rosenberg & Farrell (1976) stress this situation as one that endangers the well-being of the middle-aged man, who no longer can re-ly upon parents (who may be ill or have died already) or cultural "elders" for encouragement, assurance, direction, or wisdom. It may even be that the necessity of maintaining the "strong male image" is the source of midlife stress (Lowenthal & Chiriboga, 1972).

Morale often plummets in middle age in the absence of concrete prob-lems (Bourque & Back, 1969; Rogers, 1974). This may be due to the great ex-pectations one has had in anticipation of middle age. Research bears out this assumption, for most adults project the peak of life to occur during middle age (Back & Bourque, 1970; Bourque & Back, 1969), yet reaching the peak of one's life is accompanied by other, less pleasant, effects. Bourque & Back (1969) point out that once the adults realize they have peaked, they also realize that the remainder of their lives will proceed along a decline. They also note that, although they have reached their own heights, so have all their peers, who may have achieved more glamorous heights, thereby detracting from their own. Finally, Bardwick (1978) asserts that middle-aged adults begin to view themselves as less unique than they had when young, as they review their lives at this stage of adult development. Their problems, as well as their joys, are and often have been the same as those of others, diminishing the pride that they may take in their struggles and accomplishments.

Measuring the quality of life of middle-aged adults, hence, can be dif-ficult, for while some of their problems are concrete, others are more subtle or under the surface. Additionally, it may be that the quality of life of middle-aged men is affected only within certain groups, such as those with certain per-sonality characteristics, specific past experiences (Lowenthal & Chiriboga, 1973), or educational backgrounds (Horrocks & Mussman, 1970). Most im-portant, however, is the reluctance of many men to admit to personal doubts and anxieties (Lowenthal & Chiriboga, 1972). Lowenthal, Thurnher, et al. (1975) add that, while middle-aged men are highly stressed, they also appear least preoccupied by this stress on an overt level, thereby reducing the tendency to report personal troubles. Perhaps they feel that they, as responsible adults, are prohibited from expressing deeply felt anxieties and needs. It is not surprising, therefore, that the men in one study (Thurnher, 1976) were able to reveal dependency needs and nurturant desires only on projective, not objective, measures. Rosenberg & Farrell (1976) simply conclude that mature, middle-aged men do not feel they have the freedom or right to express or display their vulnerability; hence, their problems may be even greater than admitted by the man or recognized by others. Nevertheless, the changes of middle age are detected continually in life-span studies, which are discussed in the following section.

Alterations at Middle Age

Research that has not focused specifically on any one age group in particular has uncovered shifts, among respondents in their 40s, in response patterns and their interrelationships, on a wide variety of measures (see; for example, Andrews & Withey, 1976; Campbell et al., 1976; Frenkel-Brunswik, 1968; Gould, 1972; Horrocks & Mussman, 1970). Usually, this has taken the form of a shift in responses from population norms, or from normative response patterns established by younger or older groups. It appears, therefore, that middle age is qualitatively different from earlier or later adulthood. This idea is confirmed in a study of retrospective accounts by elderly men of their own middle age (Jackson, 1974). These men described their middle years (between the ages of about 40 and 50) as a unique period of their lives, in which they maximized their accomplishments, made their major, serious decisions, and consolidated the final direction they wanted their lives to take.

The transitional and often unstable middle age years, in turn, have been compared to the personal unrest and change that occur during adolescence (Borland, 1978; Fried, 1976; Vaillant, 1977). The term "middlescence" has even been used by numerous writers and researchers. Fried (1976) finds parallels between the teen and middlescent in terms of their emotional instability, hormonal shifts, introspectiveness, and search for the new roles and commitments that will dominate the next stage of life. The comparison stops here, however, for the developmental tasks and social circumstances facing the middle-aged adult are quite different in form and function from earlier stages of life. The adult must deal with new health concerns, with the reality of mortality, with self-assessing in the context of past and future directions, with resolving certain personal contradictions, and with assuming responsibility for the upcoming generation. Each of these features of middle age is discussed in turn.

Health. Middle-aged men do not suddenly experience a rapid decline in health. The majority are healthy enough to carry on daily activities and work to capacity at their jobs (Jaffe, 1971). However, with increasing years there is a continual aging process, so that by middle age the body does become less predictable, stamina diminishes, susceptibility increases, and a youthful appearance becomes harder to maintain (Borland, 1978). Rogers (1974) suggests that by middle age the man first experiences an emotional reaction to this decline, which may have begun gradually perhaps a decade earlier. (For example, by the time the adult has reached age 30, hardening of the arteries can be detected.) Brim (1976) also notes that certain hormonal changes occur by middle age that certainly may have repercussions in emotional and physical well-being.

Overall, biological shifts, though gradual, can provide a dramatic cue for the middle-aged man that indicates to him he is beginning to age (Neugarten, 1968b). Neugarten & Datan (1974) note that these changes are more telling for the man than the woman; for as the husband becomes concerned with changes in his bodily functions, his wife concurrently shows concern not for her own, but for her husband's health. This finding corresponds to survey research results that show that among adults aged 45 to 65 years, health is a more important predictor of life satisfaction for men than for women (Mancini, 1978).

Mortality. While most middle-aged men do remain in reasonable health, there is a drastic increase in the death rate during middle age. Among men aged 45 to 64, the mortality rate is 6 times what it had been 20 years earlier (Neugarten & Datan, 1974). If nothing else, this statistic may act as the stimulus that causes the middle-aged man to face mortality as a real and personal issue. The adult comes to realize in middle age that life is half over and death is not as far off as it once had seemed (Brim, 1976; Jaques, 1965; Rogers, 1974). One's attitude toward time shifts as a result. Neugarten (1968b, 1976) describes this shift as one from "time-since-birth" to "time-left-to-live." Data collected by Gould (1972) characterize this shift in two stages: (1) from ages 35 to 43 there appears to be an equal focus on past, present, and future and (2) from 43 to 50 years there appears to be an acceptance of the finitude of time and a feeling of relief along with this acceptance. By age 50 the present becomes the most important time dimension for providing the framework of one's life. Jaques (1965) has made a case for viewing the inevitability of one's death as *the* crucial midlife issue; however, whether this is the pivotal issue or only a secondary effect of middle age, it does indicate a major shift in the perspective of how one views one's life.

Self-Assessment. More crucial, it seems, is a process of inner assessment and self-evaluation that middle-aged adults experience (Brim, 1976; Clausen, 1972; Neugarten, 1968a, 1973, 1976; Rosenberg & Farrell, 1976). Neugarten has termed this general process as "interiority," whereby adults, by their mid 40s, turn inward as they examine their lives, their attitudes, their places in society, and their commitments to others. Self-knowledge is the result. Other researchers discuss this process in terms of (1) the existential questions that middle-aged adults begin to confront (Gould, 1972) and (2) the conscious reconstruction of their past (Lowenthal, Thurnher, et al., 1975) in order to achieve a better resolution of the present and the future that remains. Bardwick (1978) asserts that the inner examination of middle age results from the lack of external change in the lives of middle-aged adults; however, Neugarten (1976), who so often champions the impact of environment on personal development, asserts that interiority is relatively independent of adaptation or purposive behavior in the external world. It is a natural, predictable, developmental event.

In light of this process of inner assessment, discussed so commonly in life-span literature, self-respect would be expected to be a major value in the lives of middle-aged adults. It is ultimately the self to whom one must answer by the time one has reached maturity. Correspondingly, scrutiny of the tables that appear in Rokeach's (1973) book on the measurement of values reveals that between ages 30 and 49, the value of self-respect is chosen first more often than any other value of its kind, thus providing support for the idea that by middle age the self becomes the major authority in one's life. The adult, at this time, is also responsible for others, including both those younger and those older who are in need. The middle-aged adult, in turn, becomes a prime authority figure and therefore requires approval first and foremost from the self.

Resolving Personal Contradictions. The growing primacy of the self and the examination and judgment of one's life is actually a dual process. The adult attempts to come to terms with the self, but he also attempts to come to terms with the polarities and contradictions of life (Levinson, 1978). Rewards are also dual: self-understanding and an enhanced relationship with the wider social and physical world. He accepts life's contradictions as a part of reality, which need oppress him no longer with either/or choices. Riegel (1973) describes this enlightened state as the most mature stage of cognition achieved by the adult. Perhaps it is the accumulation of experience with life and the need to integrate this experience in a coherent manner during midlife self-assessment that eventually leads to a sense of comfort, not conflict, with the contradictions that living brings. A younger man has neither the experience nor the internal need to undergo this integrative process.

Levinson (1978) identifies the polar concepts integrated by middle age as young/old, destruction/creation, attachment/separateness, and masculine/feminine. These eventually become accepted features of the self and the world through the middle-age transition. Jaques (1965) also characterizes the process as one of "working through" the "depressive position" of midlife, ultimately resulting in a "further strengthening of the capacity to accept and tolerate conflict and ambivalence" (p. 513). Certainly this internal resolution results in a feeling of being more securely at peace with oneself and one's world.

Of particular interest during this transitional phase is the resolution of the masculine/feminine polarity. Around middle age, members of each sex begin to express those traits previously missing from their lives and more prevalent in the other sex (Brim, 1976; Jung, 1933; Neugarten & Gutmann, 1968). Men can become more dependent and sensitive to others. Women can become more independent, nourishing a drive toward mastery.

Several research results confirm the occurrence of a sex-role crossover. One study showed, for example, that men aged 41 to 60 years were more highly androgynous than men who were younger (Hyde & Phillis, 1979). A study conducted in Israel found that an orientation toward achievement significantly decreased after the 40s (Shanan & Sharon, 1965), and research by Lowenthal and her colleagues have indicated that middle-aged men foresee a decrease in instrumental and material values, while at the same time they reveal strong dependency and nurturance needs in projective measures (Lowenthal, Thurnher, et al., 1975; Thurnher, 1974). The researchers also found that, among their middle-aged men, not only were interpersonal and expressive values most preferred, but they were related highly and positively to life satisfaction. The opposite held for instrumental values.

Fiske (1977) concluded that the middle-aged man eventually wearies of continual self-assertion, a burden he has had to bear all his adulthood years. He also regrets the fact that he has sacrificed his emotional and interpersonal life in the name of masculine self-assertion and achievement in the external world. Rubin (1979), in a similar vein, discusses the regret among fathers whose children have grown and are on their way out of the home for having missed out on the time they could have spent nurturing their children and relating to them in a deeper, interpersonal way. By middle age, the polarities of assertive male and dependent female therefore begin to dissolve; it may be hoped that this enriches both personal lives and lives in interaction.

Generativity. At the same point in time when the middle-aged man is confronted with the task of self-assessment and integration of polar ideals, the life-span literature consistently points to the interest newly taken in guiding the young. Frenkel-Brunswik (1968), for example, states that around age 45 ideals and conscience overshadow biological and individual needs. Neugarten (1968b) discusses the middle-aged adult's enhanced sensitivity to social position. She resolves the seeming contradiction between interiority and social awareness as major components of middle-aged behavior by concluding that "self-utilization" becomes a prominent drive in middle age; interest in the next generation, be it one's children or colleagues entering the work environment, provides the opportunity for utilizing one's self-knowledge and social experience (Brim, 1976; Levinson, 1978; Neugarten, 1973). In this way the middle-aged adult can contribute to the maintenance and perpetuation of the social system in a highly responsible manner.

For this reason, Erikson's (1950, 1977) concept of the adult crisis, "generativity versus stagnation or self-absorption," is useful for characterizing this period of life. If middle-aged adults come to terms with themselves and their world, they free themselves to contribute to the social world in a more fulfilling manner. If they simply wallow in a painful soul-searching process, never quite able to accept themselves and the lives they are living, they will tend to stagnate, unable ever to shift focus from self to other, to the detriment of both.

The Benefits of Middle Age

In spite of the problems, described on the preceding pages, that the middle-aged man must attempt to cope with, this same period of life also has the potential of bringing great rewards. Certainly men in middle age confront multiple internal and external pressures, yet they also are comparatively well off and are aware of this relative status (Kerckhoff, 1976). The middle-aged adult, while coming to terms with mortality and contradiction, also is relieved eventually of the pressures of a young family and of work achievement. Responsibility in the work arena may be at a high, but the initial pressure to climb the ladder of success starting from the bottom rung has diminished gradually. He can relax a bit more, use untapped talents, and concentrate more upon being himself (Andrews & Withey, 1976; Borland, 1978; Deutscher, 1968; Neugarten, 1968b).

Concurrently, middle age is a time of maximum capacity and influence (Borland, 1978; Neugarten, 1968b). Skills that have been developed until this point in life can be exercised with great expertise and receive appropriate social rewards. Enhanced self-knowledge contributes to this satisfying state of being. Accordingly, Neugarten (1968b) reports that most middle-aged adults have little desire to be young again.

Throughout the transition to middle age, difficult as it may be, change can be viewed in a positive light. The individual who perceives personal deficiencies still has the opportunity to improve (Brim, 1976; Thurnher, 1974), for even at middle age the environment continues to reward boldness, risk, and the energy exerted toward self-improvement (Neugarten, 1973). Most men adapt gradually to the turmoil of the middle-age transition (Jaffe, 1971). Bardwick (1978) asserts that those who emerge strongest are those who have developed a secure direction for their future. Brim (1976) suggests that the transition occurring at middle age once experienced, leaves many men happier than they were when younger.

Hence, it is no surprise that many independent writers and researchers have described the decade that follows this transition as one in which the man has "mellowed" (see, for example, Gould, 1972; Lowenthal, Thurnher, et al., 1975); moreover, while Vaillant (1977) asserts that the 50s are a quieter time in life than are the 40s, Lowenthal & Chiriboga (1972) take note that men averaging age 51 characterize the present as including more high points in their lives than any other time since adolescence. Only longitudinal research, however, will reveal whether those who experience a stormy middle-age transition fare better or worse in the quieter age of the 50s than those who experience little or no midlife change.

Work and the Middle-Aged Man

There is probably no social role more central to the identity of the male adult than his occupation (Clausen, 1972; Lowenthal, Thurnher, et al., 1975). Participation in the work arena not only occupies the majority of a man's time and attention, but it also conveys to the individual his developmental status as an adult, including the onset of middle age (Neugarten, 1968b).

Middle-aged men comprise the most important segment of the working population. They are the most stable group of workers and display the lowest rates of unemployment (Jaffe, 1971; Mayer, 1969). They occupy the highest-status jobs, are in positions of seniority and authority, and earn a higher income than men at other ages within their respective social classes (Borland, 1978; Jaffe, 1971). Jaffe (1971) notes that there is no convincing evidence indicating that the skills of middle-aged men or their educational backgrounds are obsolete. In fact, most research points to the enhanced cognitive skills of the middle-aged man as applied to the work setting. He often has developed his intellectual capacities to their fullest and is able to delegate responsibilities, conceptualize wide issues in terms of their basic components, deal with contradiction, and make decisions with greatest efficiency (Birren, 1970; Borland, 1978; Neugarten, 1968b).

The Peak

Clearly, the middle-aged man is at the peak of his working career; however, once he realizes that this is the peak, for the very same reason he may panic. By middle age the man is at a plateau; further advancement is unlikely. At best, he may make a lateral shift; or he may proceed on a downward curve. Studies of adulthood uniformly document this ambiguous position of the middle-aged man, whether he comes from a high-status or low-status occupation (Borland, 1978; Brim, 1976; Clausen, 1972; Fiske, 1977; Jaffe, 1971; Mayer, 1969). Often this situation stimulates the adult to examine his career by focusing on past career decisions and weighing future options (Brim, 1976; Jaffe, 1971; Levinson, 1978; Lowenthal, Thurnher, et al., 1975; Mayer, 1969). Nevertheless, the man often finds himself in a bind. If he has not achieved what he had dreamed, there is little chance now to realize the dream, but if he has reached the heights of success, he may regret the sacrifices he made along the way and find the rewards of his current success to be less than he had anticipated.

Most studies indicate that this period in the work career of the middle-aged man occurs around the 40s. Note is often made, however, concerning the differences in timing among men holding white-collar positions requiring advanced education and men in blue-collar positions requiring little education. Generally, workers at less prestigious jobs reach their peak earlier than those who hold more professional and managerial positions (Clausen, 1972; Jaffe, 1971; Mayer, 1969). Most often, the peak of a manual worker is reached by age 40, whereas jobs requiring more education leave room for advancement even during the 40s. Nevertheless, the evidence shows that the majority simply "hold on" during this decade of life (Jaffe, 1971).

Men occupying both high- and low-prestige jobs at this time often express discontent concerning their careers. Kerckhoff (1976) reports survey results indicating that about one-half of the middle-aged managers interviewed expressed a desire to change occupations. Lowenthal & Chiriboga (1972) report that less than one-quarter of the middle-aged men they interviewed stated that their work was a current source of satisfaction. Jaffe (1971) labels this period of discontent as the "Middle Years Problem" and suggests that the following is the solution for the man who is facing the middle-age dilemma: "He either must give up his aspirations, sublimate them into non-job activities such as labor union activities, or the company bowling team, or become neurotic" (p. 80).

Options at Work

Deemphasis. Given the choices just mentioned, most research indeed indicates not neurosis but a deemphasis of work and career among middle-aged men (Fiske, 1977; Mayer, 1969). For example, Clausen (1976), reporting on longitudinal studies at Berkeley and Oakland that concentrate primarily on a middle-class sample, states that, whereas most men aged 38 expected career advancement, less than half aged 48 to 50 had similar expectations. By age 50, the men who were followed longitudinally had come to terms with the jobs they had: their satisfaction with their careers no longer was contingent on their occupational level. Clausen (1972) also notes that by the 40s decade, when the man seriously reconsiders the costs that his competitive goals have on his personal life, he may even heave a sigh of relief when he is passed over

for promotion. Although his ego may suffer a shock, he now can orient himself to a world beyond work. Jaffe (1971) more colorfully describes the desire
by some for a simpler life and the contentment to be an "Indian brave" instead of rising to "Chief" (p. 43). Additionally, at this period of time, the
blue-collar worker may be deemphasizing the role of work in his life as he an-
ticipates and plans for his retirement in the near future.

Overall, it appears that the value of competition in the work arena is
carefully reevaluated by the middle-aged man (Kerckhoff, 1976). This suggestion is supported as well by the findings discussed in the preceding section
on the quality of life, where during middle age the man often projects a decline in instrumental values for himself and diminishes his orientation toward
achievement as his major self-defining characteristic.

Reemphasis. For some men, however, work does remain central and all
consuming. In such cases work may be viewed as the last chance the individual
has to achieve success as well as security in life (Gould, 1972; Thurnher, 1974).
A study by Bardwick (1978) reveals another possible reason for total dedica-
tion to the job. The successful men aged 33 to 49 years whom she studied held
all things in life as secondary to work. Total concentration on work, however,
also affords the individual the opportunity to deny more personal inner feelings and to avoid the introspectiveness so common to middle age. Perhaps
these men, at some level, wished to put off a period of self-assessment by ded-
icating themselves to the world of work in a concentrated, driven way.

The Social Scene at Work. For most, however, if the work itself is no longer
the primary means for self-definition and satisfaction in life, other aspects of
the work setting may be coming into prominence. One of these aspects is the
interpersonal side of the job environment. For example, Andrews & Withey
(1976) find that, in their national survey sample, job items are related more
highly to feelings about helping others among men aged 45 to 59 than among
other age groups. Levinson (1978) highlights this aspect of work in terms of
the mentor–protégé relationship that becomes important to the individual
around the age of 40. He describes this relationship as "one of the most significant relationships available to men in middle adulthood" (p. 253). Instead
of a focus on self-advancement, the man at middle age, who already has
reached his senior status, can satisfy his desire for generativity (described in
the preceding section) by means of guiding the careers of members of the upcoming generation. It is likely that this aspect of work constitutes one of the
strongest appeals of the job setting for the middle-aged man, for, in contrast
to the positive description of the interpersonal draw of work given by Levinson, Fiske (1977) reports that those middle-aged adults bored with work also
tend to withdraw from on-the-job relationships.

Overall, it appears that the middle-aged man, in the course of taking stock of his life, reorganizes his priorities. Work is enjoyed primarily when it loses its competitive edge, and on-the-job goals broaden in their personal and social benefits. Skills that have been developed may be enjoyed in and of themselves, and a sense of generativity is gained by imparting these skills to others.

Family and the Middle-Aged Man

The preceding pages have described some of the difficulties encountered by the man as he makes his transition to middle age. It follows that there are bound to be repercussions in family life. Much of the family and life-span literature attests to this point. Family life during this period has been described as stormy and tension-packed (Brim, 1976; Chilman, 1968). Not only is the husband–father at a turning point in life, but so are the growing children and the wife whose primary role as mother is coming to a close (Chilman, 1968). The middle-aged man also may experience role "strain" at this point in time, as he attempts to reintegrate his multiple roles in the context of work, community, and home (Rollins & Cannon, 1974).

The Empty-Nest Syndrome

The most popular paradigm used to describe the family during middle age has been the analysis of parental well-being in terms of the time before and the time after the children leave home, that is to say, before and after the "nest" is emptied. Most accounts of this process indicate that, prior to the exit of children, satisfaction and in particular marital satisfaction, reaches an all-time low; but once the children are gone satisfaction takes a turn for the better and the marriage relationship begins to thrive (Borland, 1978; Brim, 1976; Burr, 1970; Campbell et al., 1976; Chilman, 1968; Deutscher, 1968, 1969; Lowenthal, Thurnher, et al., 1975). This switch has been attributed to several factors, including increased freedom and decreased financial responsibilities, an enhanced sense of accomplishment due to having completed the job of raising one's children, and a new level of interaction between husband and wife, whose unique personalities now can take precedence over the former, more rigidly defined roles of mother and father (Clausen, 1972; Deutscher, 1968, 1969).

It is questionable, however, whether the actual physical departure of the child alone can completely account for these changes. A child living within the home actually may be more independent of parents than a child living apart from parents yet receiving financial and emotional aid. The parent role certainly is not terminated just because the child is not living in the home

(Borland, 1978). Axelson (1960) shows, for example, that there is no difference in satisfaction, in various domains of living, between parents of children
under 18 at home and parents of children who have married. Serlin (1979),
too, has found minimal differences in well-being between parental and post-
parental groups. Rollins & Cannon (1974) note that even if a drop in marital
satisfaction occurs prior to launching children from the home, the drop is very
small, and marital satisfaction remains high nonetheless.

More importantly, the bulk of research evidence indicates that men are
affected much less by family life-cycle stages than are their wives. Even the
way men perceive their lives is in tune with the outer world of work and not
the age of their children (Neugarten, 1968b; Rollins & Feldman, 1970). For
example, Glenn (1975), in an examination of six national surveys, has shown
that, while women display increased happiness posparentally, the findings for
men are inconsistent and of small magnitude. Lowenthal, Thurnher, et al.
(1975) correspondingly report that fewer than one-third of the middle-aged
men they interviewed considered the launching of children from the home as
an important life transition. It simply may be that if the empty-nest paradigm
for the study of adult development is of any utility, it is in the context of
female adult development, or of the development of conjugal relations between women and men, and not the adult development of men.

Problems of Parenthood

The above conclusion just reached is not meant to suggest that relationships
with one's adolescent and young adult children have no impact upon the
middle-aged father. Generally, the evidence suggests that the relationships
between middle-aged men and their older children are tense (Borland, 1978;
Brim, 1976; Burr, 1970; Chilman, 1968). Often the attitudes and value systems held by parent and child are at odds, with little effort on the part of
either party to compromise his position. Others have suggested that the middle-aged parent begins to envy his youthful offspring (or, for that matter,
youth as a whole), especially in terms of their strength, their energy, and their
multiple options for living (Fried, 1976; Levinson, 1978). In addition, the
problems with which the adolescent child must cope, such as sexuality, interpersonal relations, and a search for personal identity, may have the effect of
raising anew the very same internal conflicts within the middle-aged parent,
touching off the process of inner assessment and painful self-analysis (Chilman, 1968; Vaillant, 1977). Finally, the adolescent child seeks freedom from
the parent, previously so all-powerful in word and deed. The parent, consequently, must lessen his control of his nearly adult child and accept this limitation of power on a permanent basis (Brim, 1976).

The issue of parent–child conflict, however, in most cases should not be
overplayed. Lowenthal, Thurnher, et al. (1975), for example, report that,
while approximately 75 percent of men middle-aged and above retrospective-

ly report some degree of conflict with their children, the majority also are quick to state the moderate nature of the event and their positive feelings about their children. The men in their study also did not view the departure of their last child from home as constituting any problem at all (Lowenthal & Chiriboga, 1972). Most interestingly, their feelings about their children had absolutely no impact upon their psychological well-being during middle age (Thurnher, 1976).

These findings mesh well with the results of the longitudinal data described by Clausen (1976). He reports that, for men between 40 and 50 years old, emphasis on the parental role begins to diminish. Overall, therefore, it appears that the role of parenting in middle age is not a major contributor, in either a positive or negative direction, to the well-being of the middle-aged man. It does appear, however, that the marriage plays a more central role in the life of the middle-aged man, for Lowenthal, Thurnher, et al. (1975) report that, when faced with ambiguous pictures of the Thematic Apperception Test, the responses of middle-aged men are more concerned with a conjugal relationship and not a parental one, although both types of responses are potentially equally likely.

Middle-Aged Marriage

Given that the marital relationship is important at middle age, there are mixed reports in the literature as to how solid the relationship is at this stage in life. Kerckhoff (1976) summarizes previous findings as indicating either marital "bliss" or marital "blahs" during middle age (p. 9). Some studies report increased marital satisfaction in middle age, attributed to factors such as increased joint activities, sympathy, and affection (see, for example, Axelson, 1960; Gould, 1972). Other studies report increased discontent with marriage at middle age, attributed especially to the boredom of husband and wife with their relationship and life together (see, for example, Borland, 1978; Kerckhoff, 1976). These reports, however, are difficult to assess, for Kerckhoff (1976) observes that often, when marriages are defined as happy, it simply may indicate lack of overt discord between husband and wife and disregard for the fact that the marriage itself is lifeless. He describes these types of relationships as "easy to endure and easy to ignore" (p. 9).

There are specific problems that do arise in marriages during middle age. Lowenthal, Thurnher, et al.'s (1975) middle-aged subjects present a unique set of marital problems, but note should be taken that the findings from their study have not been replicated by other researchers and thus may be confined to their lower-middle and working-class sample. Specifically, they found that the wives were more critical of their husbands than any other age group; but, while the husbands stressed their wive's positive points, they also admitted to their own inadequacies in fulfilling their wives' expectations and emotional needs (Lowenthal, Thurnher, et al., 1975; Thurnher, 1976). The researchers found that the middle-aged men continued to perceive family positions in terms of the well-defined roles of husband–provider and wife–mother, yet these men were painfully aware that economic security was not sufficient in ensuring their wives' emotional happiness. This point is illustrated best by the men's responses to projective measures, where sensitivity to emotional and affiliative themes was dominant.

There are several plausible explanations for the findings observed by Lowenthal and her colleagues. The men may very well be in the midst of the midlife transition, coming to terms with facets of their personality not previously expressed, such as their need for affiliation. Yet they have not shaken themselves fully loose from their traditional role of the family provider who has control of the family and of their (men's) own emotional state. Secondly, the wives in this sample were having a particularly trying time in adjusting to the fact that their youngest child was about to be launched from the home. They were more depressed than women of other ages in the wider sample. This unpleasant personal state may have influenced the responses of their husbands, who felt helpless in aiding their wives through this difficult period. Finally, the tension between, on the one hand, ascribing to rigid role definitions for describing family members and, on the other, the less visible need to relate to these members on a more personal level may be a characteristic of working-class samples and not the more educated middle- and upper-middle classes (Bernstein, 1970; Rubin, 1976).

Nevertheless, a component of this situation that is more clearly apparent in other studies concerns the sex-role crossover among middle-aged adults. Men become more attuned to affiliative needs and women to their need to achieve in a world beyond the home. Brim (1976) has hypothesized that in this situation it is often the husband who loses out. In light of the fact that the largest percentage of full-time working women are middle aged, and especially women in their 40s (Jaffe, 1971), a large supply of middle-aged housewives are eliminated from the home. No longer is the woman available to cheer her husband from the sidelines, to offer abundant affection and support, and give him a sense of personal value. Lowenthal & Weiss (1976) correspondingly suggest that their middle-aged male respondents tended to receive less "pampering" from their wives than they had desired over time, much to their disappointment.

Overall, the transition to middle age involves a renegotiation between marital partners as to their mutual relationship and the personal contribution each member has to offer. This will usually result, according to Clausen (1972), in either a realistic acceptance of each other as partners in a relationship, or the painful recognition of an unsatisfactory marriage, for Clausen reports that by the age of 50 few expect that their spouse will change.

The outcome of this situation appears pivotal to the personal well-being of the man at middle age. The marriage is often the strongest and most intimate human relationship experienced by the man, who typically fails to establish mutual relationships of equal intensity with friends or other family members (Lowenthal & Robinson, 1976). A striking finding reported by Thurnher (1976) confirms this assumption at middle age: positive feelings toward the wife by the middle-aged man appear to be associated with *general* life satisfaction, although not necessarily with his immediate mood from day-to-day.

Social Relationships
and the Middle-Aged Man

Relationships with others in everyday living are an important component of the quality of life. They provide a sense of continuity to the individual and a stable anchor for personality and self-development, especially at times of rapid change (Clausen, 1972; Hess, 1972). Little is known about the social relations of the middle-aged man. No study to date has focused exclusively on this issue. Several studies, however, have included one or several variables concerning the friendship patterns of men. The results of these studies reveal inconsistent findings, which are described within this section.

Friendship: Pro and Con

Several studies have suggested that the onset of middle age provokes an increased interest in friends and social activities (Gould, 1972; Horrocks & Mussman, 1970). Survey research has shown that during the 40s respondents begin to display a new cluster of items representative of their feelings about social relationships. They express a strong interest in jobs and community relationships and an enhanced appreciation of their neighborhood and friends. Lowenthal provides a more clinical observation concerning interest in social relations during middle age. She states that during this time in life men begin to regret the way in which they denied themselves the pleasure of interpersonal ties at the expense of material goals. This is illustrated most strikingly by results from projective measures, where a strong desire for nurturance surfaces at middle age (Fiske, 1977; Lowenthal, Thurnher, et al., 1975).

Ambivalent Associations

Lowenthal also finds that men score lowest in friendship participation during their middle years. They perceive the issue of friendship in a highly simplistic manner, lacking in cognitive and emotional depth (Lowenthal, Thurnher, et al., 1975). Other research has led to the conclusion that the draw toward friendship is highly ambivalent during middle age. Gould (1972) has found that, despite renewed interest in them at about ages 43 to 50, friendship ties remain fairly superficial in nature and maintain an element of competitiveness. Perhaps this has to do with the idea that the middle-aged man is ex-

pected to have reached a peak in life. He may be comparing continually his
success in life with that achieved by others his age. This can hinder the establishment with peers of close interpersonal ties that will be mutually supportive,
especially if the man becomes envious of the accomplishments displayed by
his so-called "friends."

An additional impediment to the development and maintenance of
friendship ties in middle age is the complex pattern of multiple roles played
by the middle-aged man in home, community, and work. Hess (1972) suggests that the resulting friendships are likely to be "differentiated" and
"compartmentalized" during the middle-aged period (p. 370). This situation inhibits the formation of friendships that transcend the boundaries of
these various roles.

Individual Differences

The meager body of literature that addresses the problem of friendships
among men at middle age allows one to conclude only that there must be a
wide range of individual differences in the desire for and participation in
social relationships at middle age. Lowenthal & Weiss (1976), for example,
report that for middle-aged men there is a strong association between mutual
relationships and stress: the greater the participation in close relationships,
the less preoccupation with stress. Unfortunately, those men most overtaken
by personal stress were least able to maintain these mutual relations.

Results such as these point to the idea that social relationships can supply
a much-needed resource to the man at middle age. Survey research by Mancini (1978) has shown additionally that friendship during middle age is a
more important predictor of life satisfaction for men than for women. Whereas women, throughout the life cycle, participate in multiple interpersonal
relationships, men maintain fewer intimate ties with friends and relatives in
general. In times of stress, therefore, friendship patterns may fluctuate more
for men, facilitating the formation of ties or impeding the mobilization of
much-needed social supports. It also may be that social relations grow in importance (whether they actually are experienced or conspicuously lacking) in
the life of the middle-aged man because there is a need to share one's soul-
searching efforts with others undergoing similar transitions, and because of
the need to round out an overly impersonal, achievement-orientation to life.

A Plan for the Study of
Middle-Aged Men

The review of the literature in preceding pages concerning men at middle age
leads to a single conclusive statement: *the transition to middle age constitutes
a unique period of time in the adult life of the male.* Firm conclusions con-

cerning the quality of life experience, work, family, and social relationships of middle-aged men are lacking. The research is spotty, the results ambiguous. No study to date has focused exclusively on men at middle age.

For this reason, the present study attempts to fill this gap. The pages that follow describe the method and results of an exploratory study, utilizing national survey data, of men during their transition to middle age. It explores initially their quality of life experience, followed by an analysis of their work, family, and social relationships and the contribution of each of these domains to the well-being of the individual. In all analyses, middle-aged men are compared with men at other stages of life, in order to assess the similarities and differences between the two groups. Throughout, the analysis is conducted under a single guiding hypothesis: *ages 40 to 49 years in the life of the adult male comprise a major transitional period that is reflected in the quality of life experience, with repercussions in the worlds of work, family, and social relationships.*

2

A Method for the Study of Middle-Aged Men

This study examines, through the analysis of national survey data, the transition to middle age. This chapter describes the design and data collection procedures of the national survey. The particular subsample within the survey that serves as the focus of the present investigation (that is, men who are in their 40s) then is described. After this, the analysis strategy is outlined, including both the form of the measures and the statistical techniques appropriate to their analysis. Finally, the structure of the results is discussed.

The Survey

The Interview: A Study of Modern Living

The survey data examined in this investigation were obtained from a representative national sample of adults aged 21 and older interviewed in 1976. The respondents, who were interviewed in their own homes, were told the survey was a "Study of Modern Living" (Douvan, Veroff, & Kulka, 1976). The survey was described to respondents as an attempt to examine the "stresses and strains" of modern life and the possible problems engendered by the "rapid pace" of living in modern society. The interview was completely voluntary, and respondents were assured that any questions they were unable or unwilling to answer would be skipped. The interview, of about 90 minutes' duration, then proceeded to cover a wide variety of topics, including the social roles, mental health, and coping strategies of the individual.

    The "Study of Modern Living" was designed to assess nationwide information on what normal Americans think of their health (Veroff, Douvan, & Kulka, in press). The survey was actually a replication of a similar national survey taken in 1957, also conducted to gauge the mental health of normal American adults, but the 1976 study added new questions and measures. (Results of the 1957 survey have been published in two books: *Americans View Their Mental Health*, by Gurin, Veroff, & Feld, 1960; and *Marriage and Work in America*, by Veroff & Feld, 1970).

Funded by the National Institute of Mental Health, the 1976 survey provided a means to assess the quality of life and its social indicators within the nation. Authors of the survey (Douvan et al., 1976) were committed to an assessment of subjective mental health based upon multiple criteria; therefore they constructed the interview so that many dimensions of the quality of life were tapped. The interview, which asked both closed and open-ended questions, evaluated the individual's feelings and sources of well-being; the social roles of marriage, parenthood, and work; social supports; motivation; values; symptoms; formal help-seeking; and demographic information. Hence, with a multiple-criteria approach, specific sites of mental-health troubles could be pinpointed, as well as sources of individual strengths and coping mechanisms.

Trained and experienced interviewers from the field staff of the Survey Research Center at the University of Michigan's Institute for Social Research conducted the interviews. Direct contact by the interviewers was preceded by a letter to each potential respondent. Interviewers were provided with question-by-question instructions about the survey, and they additionally assured respondents of the confidentiality of the information obtained. The typical interviewer was a white middle-aged woman, although there was an effort to match interviewers and respondents by race. Postinterview questionnaires indicated that most respondents found the interviews to be an interesting experience, in spite of the lengthy hour and a half (Veroff, Douvan, & Kulka, in press).

Sampling Design

The national sample interviewed for the "Study of Modern Living" was drawn by the Sampling Section of the Survey Research Center by a multistage probability area sampling design described by Kish & Hess (1965).

Briefly, this procedure first identified within the coterminous United States primary sampling points of Standard Metropolitan Sampling Areas, single counties, and county groups within the Northeast, North-Central, South, and Western regions of the United States. Successive subdivisions of these areas were conducted in accordance with sampling probabilities proportionate to their populations, initially, and with equal probabilities in the final stages. At the final stage, households were selected and one resident among

the eligible members was chosen randomly to be interviewed. If, following re-
peated calls, no one was home, or if the designated respondent was absent or
unable or unwilling to be interviewed, no substitution was made.

For the "Study of Modern Living," 71 percent of the designated respondents were interviewed successfully. The total achieved sample for the
survey numbered 2264 respondents (960 men and 1304 women). Additionally, a comparison of the "Study of Modern Living" sample with the 1970 census and the 1976 Current Population Survey indicated no substantial devia-
tions for major demographic characteristics (Klingel & Kulka, 1978).

It should be noted that, because the sampling procedure used in this
study is based upon a multistage area sampling design as opposed to simple
random sampling, the standard error is somewhat larger than those conven-
tionally used. The average design effect (which is based on the ratio of variances for complex and simple random sampling) for this survey, however, is
relatively close to 1.0, suggesting that the effect upon the standard error due
to the multistage design is quite small.

The Study Sample

Men in Families

The transition to middle age in the course of normative life-cycle development is the focus of the investigation. As indicated in the guiding hypothesis
outlined in Chapter 1, this transition is expected to occur among men, on
the average, between ages 40 and 49. This group of men, therefore, comprises
the major population for comparison. Men in their 40s are compared with
men of similar status, both older and younger than themselves. This status
similarity is defined by the normative social roles occupied by men in adulthood: husband and father.

There are both theoretical and pragmatic reasons for limiting the focus of
this study to men who are both married and parents. Theoretically, men who
experience the life cycle in the normative manner, marrying in young adulthood and becoming a parent thereafter, experience a qualitative difference in
lifestyle and sense of well-being than men who have never married, have
divorced, or have been widowed earlier in adulthood but have not remarried.
Andrews & Withey (1976) note, for example, that those individuals who fail
to experience the normative family life-cycle stages display a different pattern
of age differences than those who do. Pearlin & Johnson (1977) have shown
that adults who are not married are significantly more vulnerable to stress and
less likely to enjoy psychological well-being than adults who are married.
Glick (1977) additionally reports that, in spite of attention directed at rising
divorce rates in current times, married life continues to be the norm, and the
majority of men and women remarry following divorce.

Pragmatically, this results in an overwhelming majority of men during their adulthood years being both married and parents. Within the "Study of Modern Living," so few men were unmarried and childless that they comprised too small a group to compare with statistical assurance to the normative sample of married fathers. Of the 155 men in the sample aged 40 to 49, only 22 were unmarried (due to separation, divorce, widowhood, or bachelorhood), and of the 133 men who were married, only 5 had no children. These men, therefore, have been omitted from the analysis.

The decision to limit the investigation to men who are married fathers led to an additional limitation concerning the age range of the comparison group. Men who are 40 to 49 are compared in this investigation to men, similarly married and parents, ranging from 25 to 39 years and from 50 to 69 years of age. Few men either above or below the age range of 25 to 69 years are both currently married and parents (that is, those over 69 are more likely to be widowed), thereby limiting the opportunity to compare them with statistical assurance to men who are middle aged. Additionally, for stratification of analyses by the critical educational control described in the following section, there are too few men above age 69 who have had a college education to compare with the college-educated middle-aged men, once education controls are instituted.

Therefore, the sample utilized in the present study consists of men between the ages of 25 and 69 years who are currently married and parents. Table 2.1 describes the number of men in each age group from 25 to 69 years in 5-year intervals.

It is important to take note, given the parental status of the sample examined, of the approximate age levels of the children in the families of these men, and in particular of the men between 40 and 49. Table 2.2 displays the developmental levels of these children as defined by their status in school. Beginning at age 40, a firm majority of the fathers within the sample have at least one child of high-school age or above; hence, an additional descriptive characteristic of the men aged 40 to 49 within the sample under scrutiny, is that a major feature of their family structure is the presence of at least one adolescent or young adult son or daughter.

The Education Control

A study of developmental change must account for differences in social class and the corresponding social milieu. It has been suggested that men undergoing a transition to middle age have differing experiences in the timing of the transition and in their concomitant subjective well-being as a function of the social class to which they belong (Deutscher, 1968; Horrocks & Mussman, 1970; Mayer, 1969; Neugarten, 1968; Neugarten & Datan, 1974; Rosenberg & Farrell, 1976; Wilensky, 1968). Others have suggested that class is irrelevant; they assert that all men at middle age experience a shift toward introspectiveness, self-assessment, and personality reorganization (Levinson, 1978; Neugarten & Gutman, 1968). Only by comparing men of differing social classes can this issue be resolved.

Education is used in this study as the measure of social class. Previous research indicates that education is often the most powerful predictor of differences between groups of respondents (see, for example, Breytspraak, 1974; Kulka et al., 1979; Locksley, 1978; Wilensky, 1968). Education is often the single variable that correlates with nearly all other indicators of social class, such as occupation, income, and mobility. Jaffe (1971) notes that education is highly related to economic success and occupational prestige. Family income is a less useful measure for differentiating men at middle age; often the working pattern of the wife can inflate or deflate this variable.

The present investigation divides the sample of married fathers into two educational levels: (1) noncollege and (2) college educated. The noncollege-educated group consists of men who have received a high-school degree or less. Although those men who have never achieved more than a gradeschool

Table 2.1 Number of Married Fathers Aged 25–69

Age	Total	Non–College[a]	College[b]
25–29	78	44	33
30–34	76	42	34
35–39	76	43	33
40–44	65	33	32
45–49	63	39	24
50–54	37	21	16
55–59	68*	42	25
60–64	52	45	7
65–69	36	29	7

[a]Men with a High School education or less.

[b]Men with some College education or more.

* This row does not total properly because educational status was not indicated in one case.

Table 2.2   School Level of Children of Married Fathers

| Age of Father | Level of Children | |
	Gradeschool and Below	Highschool and Above
25-29	75 (98.7%)	1 (1.3%)*
30-34	69 (92.0%)	6 (7.9%)
35-39	39 (56.5%)	30 (43.5%)
40-44	12 (18.7%)	52 (81.2%)
45-49	5 (7.9%)	58 (92.1%)
50-54	2 (5.4%)	35 (94.6%)
55-59	1 (1.5%)	67 (98.5%)
60-64	0	52 (100 %)
65-69	0	35 (100 %)

*Percentages may not add up to 100, but may be one or two tenths off (that is, 99.9 or 100.1). This is due to the rounding out of numbers within the computer program.

education may constitute a particular group of interest, only 11 men aged 40 to 49 years are at this educational level; therefore, they are included within the noncollege group. The college-educated group consists of men who have received at least some college education or more. Further subdivisions of this group would result in cells too small for comparison purposes. Table 2.1 displays the number of men within each of these groups between ages 25 and 69 years. It is important to note, however, that the number of men within the college sample aged 60 to 69 is quite small, a fact which should be taken into account when examining results for men of this age. Additionally, in the tables of results in the chapters that follow, the sample sizes of each age group are not included, since they remain fairly constant for all measures.

Analysis Strategy

The exploratory study described in this book attempts to define the changes that occur in the lives of men during their 40s. This is done by examining the responses of men interviewed in 1976 concerning the "quality of their life experience," their "work," their "family," and their "social relationships."

The study is structured so that the first and most important set of questions concerns the quality of life experience at middle age. Work, family, and social relationships are examined separately thereafter, both by themselves and for their contribution to the measurement of well-being (a major component of the quality of life experience) of men in their 40s. In addition, each analysis is conducted initially for the men as a whole, followed by separate analyses for the college- and noncollege-educated groups.

The remainder of this chapter discusses more specifically the statistical techniques used for consolidating data, identifying age differences, and assessing the significance of these differences for the sample under consideration.

Construction of Indices

The "Study of Modern Living" presents the researcher with an abundance of items for analysis. Many items, however, tap into similar dimensions of the psychological state of the respondent. Several questions, for example, were asked concerning the degree to which the respondent is depressed or the degree to which he is satisfied with his occupation. In cases such as these, more powerful conclusions can be drawn when these items are consolidated into more general indices.

The construction of indices for this study is based upon several analytic steps. Initially, those items are selected from the interview questionnaire that are most relevant to an examination of the transition to middle age. Items that appear to measure dimensions within the same general domain then are grouped together. For example, items that ask about aspects of work, such as the likelihood of looking for another job, how interesting one's work is, and how often one talks with others at work, are considered potential items for the construction of indices concerning work. These items are then factor analyzed, utilizing the entire sample of men. Following rotation, items with loadings .60 or above on a single factor are considered for inclusion in an index representative of that dimension.

Other aspects of these items also are examined, however, prior to index construction. The items should behave similarly in relation to other variables and should be highly intercorrelated among themselves and with the composite variable (Babbie, 1973). The best measure of the internal consistency of the items that form the composite variable is Cronbach's alpha statistic (Cronbach, 1951). This statistic is calculated for the composite index under consideration. Following the advice of Nunnally for acceptable levels of reliability for exploratory research, such as this study, a minimum reliability coefficient of .50 or .60 is required (Nunnally, 1967). If this minimum level is reached, the composite measure is used in subsequent analyses in lieu of separate analyses for each of the items included within it.

Parametric Statistics

Once items for analysis are identified and composite variables are constructed, each of these variables is treated as a dependent variable. The dependent variables are then examined in relation to a single independent variable: age.

The age variable is constructed initially at intervals of five years for the sample of married fathers aged 25 to 69, as appears in Table 2.1. Age groups are collapsed, however, when statistically permissible, that is, when the means of the differing age groups are not significantly different. Thus, for example, men aged 25 to 39 can be compared to men aged 40 to 49; or men aged 25 to 39 and 50 to 69 can be compared together to the middle-aged group. It should be noted that the group aged 40 to 49 is referred to as the middle-aged group for the purpose of data presentation, although it actually represents the group making the *transition* to middle age. Accordingly, men aged 25 to 39 are referred to as the *younger* men, and those aged 50 to 69 as the *older* men, also for the purpose of consolidating data presentation.

As described in Appendix A and elaborated in the following chapters, most of the measures used are ordinal variables. For example, respondents may answer the question "Taking things all together, how would you say things are these days?" with a choice of "very happy," "pretty happy," or "not too happy." Clearly, responses are ordered from most to least happy, but well-defined numerical intervals between the three choices are absent. For the purposes of the present research, however, these variables are treated as interval data and analyzed by the more powerful parametric statistics which require interval data at minimum. Initially, each variable is examined by means of a one-way analysis of variance (ANOVA). The independent variable is age, and the dependent variable is the individual's response.

There are several powerful arguments offered in the statistical literature concerning the benefits of treating ordinal data as if they were interval so that parametric statistics (such as ANOVA, correlation, and regression) can be utilized. Parametric techniques of analysis are clearly superior to nonparametric techniques. Their power, retention of information about the data, and options for statistical manipulation are far greater than those of nonparametric methods (Kerlinger, 1967; Labovitz, 1967, 1970). Labovitz (1967, 1970) asserts that it is better to treat "not quite interval" scales as interval, lest much information be wasted. The small amount of error engendered by treating ordinal scales as interval is more than compensated for by the more powerful, sensitive, and clearly interpretable parametric techniques.

In addition, parametric techniques that utilize the F distribution test, such as the ANOVA, are extremely robust. They are nearly immune to even extreme violations of their assumptions of normality and homogeneity of variance (Boneau, 1960; Kerlinger, 1967; Labovitz, 1967, 1970; Lindquist,

1953). Labovitz (1967) adds that the smaller the number of cases per cell, the stronger the incentive to use the more powerful parametric tests.

Analysis of Variance. Each ordinal or interval variable, whether a composite or a single item, is analyzed by means of one-way ANOVAs, using age as the independent variable. The ANOVAs are calculated initially for the nine separate age groups at five-year intervals between 25 to 69 years of age. However, the guiding hypothesis of this study posits that ages 40 to 49 are qualitatively different from other ages. Ideally, therefore, a planned comparison ANOVA strategy would appear to be the optimal and most parsimonious technique and would involve a strategy where men in their 40s are compared with the men of other ages combined. However, planned comparisons are permissible only if the comparisons are orthogonal to one another (Hays, 1973). Since this study is exploratory, the age-group comparisons necessary for the analysis are not orthogonal; they are overlapping, and therefore planned comparisons are not possible. Specifically, the following four comparisons are indicated:

1. Men aged 40 to 49 versus men aged 25 to 39 and 50 to 69
2. Men aged 40 to 44 versus men aged 25 to 39 and 45 to 69
3. Men aged 45 to 49 versus men aged 25 to 44 and 50 to 69
4. Men aged 25 to 44 versus men aged 45 to 69

Comparison 1 is a direct reflection of the original guiding hypothesis. Comparisons 2 and 3 represent an attempt to pinpoint the site of middle-age differences during the early or late 40s. Comparison 4 directly assesses whether the 40s comprise a transitional stage by testing whether the man, as he enters his 40s, is more like those younger and, as he reaches his late 40s, is more like those older, the transition having occurred somewhere between.

Because this study is exploratory, it is essential to investigate each of these four nonorthogonal comparisons so that all possible information concerning the middle-aged group is assessed. However, following Neter & Wasserman (1974), the Group Effect Decomposition Method does provide an appropriate tool for the analysis of the four comparisons. The decomposition method is used when factor levels (age) are classified into relevant groups (40 to 49, 25 to 39, and 50 to 69) and when, as Neter & Wasserman put it, interest is in

1. Whether or not the different group means are the same, and
2. Whether or not the several factor level means within each group are the same. [pp. 459–460]

Therefore, age groups are collapsed when no significant mean differences within are found (by means of the ANOVA). They are then compared with one another (as in comparisons 1 and 4) or with the single middle-aged subgroup of interest (as in comparisons 2 and 3), using the *F*-test of significance. It is important to note that the decomposition method as used in this study provides a more stringent test than the planned comparison method, because mean differences within groups are assessed in the former method, whereas they simply are collapsed when using the planned comparison technique. A major constraint exercised in the present investigation is that age groups are collapsed only when their means are not significantly different. For all comparisons a probability value of .05 or less is considered to be indicative of a statistically significant age-group difference.

Time Series Plots. Two other descriptive techniques are used in conjunction with the ANOVA: time series plots and contingency table analysis. The first technique, time series plots, involves the treatment of the independent variable age as if it were time series data. Each year between ages 25 and 69 is treated as a single case. Means of the dependent variables for each year then are graphed on a time series plot. The horizontal axis represents age by year, and the vertical axis represents the range of scores for the dependent variable. For example, a single point represents the mean for all men aged 25, the next point the mean at age 26, and so on.

Time series data, however, allow the researcher to institute techniques that "smooth out" the resulting curve by means of a moving average and thereby achieve a clearer picture of changes in scores over time (that is, age by years). The moving average calculates the mean of not only a single point in time (or in this case, age), but that of the adjacent time points along with the point in time between them. For example, a moving average of three will calculate the mean of ages 39, 40, and 41 and plot this average score at age 40; similarly, it will calculate the mean of ages 40, 41, and 42 and plot this average score at age 41. By increasing the size of the moving average (say, from three to five to seven, and so on), the resulting curve becomes increasingly smooth. Trends are more readily apparent.

For the purposes of the present research, a moving average of seven is utilized. This means that each point plotted on the time series graph represents the mean of the age group at that point and the three adjacent means on each side. The point that is plotted at age 45, therefore, actually represents the means of ages 42, 43, 44, 45, 46, 47, and 48. In the present investigation, the moving average size of seven was chosen because the three-layer leeway on either side allows for more loosely defined boundaries of age-related changes, and, on a more pragmatic level, it produces a smooth yet interpretable curve for exploratory purposes, more so than other intervals initially examined.

Contingency Tables. Variables based upon ordinal or interval scales can be analyzed by techniques such as the ANOVA, and means can be calculated for time series analysis; however, not all the variables examined in this study are measured on either ordinal or interval scales. Several of the variables are based upon nominal categorizations. They involve the choice of several possible responses that do not represent an ordered increase or decrease on some dimension, such as happiness, symptoms, or work satisfaction. An example of a nominal variable used in this study is the choice from among nine possible categories of the respondent's most important value, be it fun and enjoyment, warm relationships, self-respect, security, or the like. In these cases, contingency table analysis, a nonparametric technique, is used. Age, the independent variable, is plotted against the dependent variable, the nominal category response. Chi-square values are calculated in order to determine whether there are significant differences among the age groups in categorical responses.

The Detection of Interactions

Correlational Analysis. The preceding section has outlined the three major descriptive techniques performed at the initial stage of data analysis: ANOVA, time series plots, the contingency table analysis. These techniques indicate whether or not middle-aged men (that is, men aged 40 to 49) differ from men at other ages on single-variable measures, be they composite variables or single items. These techniques do not indicate whether the interrelationships between these variables differ for men at middle age when compared with men younger (25 to 39 years) or older (50 to 69 years).

In order to detect the interrelationships between variables for the young, middle-aged, and older adults, correlation matrices are calculated for four differing subsamples:

1. Middle-aged men (40 to 49 years)
2. Younger men (25 to 39 years)
3. Older men (50 to 69 years)
4. All nonmiddle-aged men (25 to 39 and 50 to 69 years), a combination of 2 and 3.

These correlation matrices are calculated at each stage of the analysis; that is, the well-being variables from the quality-of-life-experience measures are intercorrelated initially, followed by the calculation of correlation matrices for (1) the work variables, both among themselves and with the well-being variables; (2) the family variables, both among themselves and with the well-being variables; and (3) the social-relationship variables, both among themselves and with the well-being variables. This sequence is done for each of the age groups just listed.

A correlation coefficient is considered for further investigation if it reaches a value of .30 or above. Although values below .30 may be statistically significant, they are not considered to be of psychological significance if they account for less than nine percent of the variance at minimum.

Once correlation coefficients of .30 or above have been isolated in the correlation matrices for either the young, middle-aged, or older subsamples, the correlations between these specific variables are tabulated and compared for each of the subsamples. For example, when a correlation of .39 is found between the variables ''work affiliation'' and ''work interest'' for the middle-aged group (40 to 49 years), it is recorded and compared with the correlation coefficients obtained among the young-adult (25 to 39 years) and older-adult (50 to 69 years) groups, which in this case are .02 and .05, respectively. In other cases, correlation values may be greater than .30 for the nonmiddle-aged group (25 to 39 and 50 to 69 years) and less than .30 for the middle-aged men.

In cases where such discrepant values are found, with correlations either much higher or much lower for middle-aged men than men who are older or younger, it is assumed that the relationship between the correlated variables is different for middle-aged men than for others. In the case just outlined, for example, it is assumed that work affiliation and work interest are more highly related at middle age than any other stage of life. Simply identifying and recording differences in correlation coefficients, however, does not indicate to the researcher whether the differences are statistically significant, rather than a product of chance alone. In order to assess the significance of these differences, therefore, two techniques are used to compare the correlation coefficients: (1) the r to z transformation formula and (2) dummy variable regression.

A Formula Comparing Correlations. When the correlation between the same two variables appears different for differing, independent populations (in this case, middle-aged men, and nonmiddle-aged men), the straightforward r to z transformation formula can be used to calculate the significance of this difference:[1]

$$z = \frac{z_1 - z_2}{\sigma(z_1 - z_2)} = \frac{z_1 - z_2}{\sqrt{\dfrac{1}{N_1 - 3} + \dfrac{1}{N_2 - 3}}}$$

[1]The values of z_1 and z_2 in the r to z transformation formula are derived from the values of the two correlation coefficients being compared (r_1 and r_2) by means of a standard r to z transformation table. The values N_1 and N_2 correspond to the size of the two independent sample populations. The resulting z score calculated by this formula is referred to a table of the normal probability distribution (Hays, 1973).

The more conservative two-tailed significance level is used in this study as the criterion for assessing the significance of correlation differences since no predictions are assumed beforehand about the direction of the differences that may occur.

If the significance of correlation differences is confirmed by means of the r to z formula, however, the researcher is left with the question of how to explain the statistical source of these differences. There are two possible reasons why the correlations differ: either the variance is higher for one of the correlation coefficients or the correlation coefficients represent relationships with different statistical slopes. In order to assess whether the slopes beween two variables differ for differing subgroups, dummy variable multiple regression provides the more powerful statistical tool. Therefore, prior to the calculation of the r to z transformation formula, regression, as described in the following section, is used in order to determine whether slopes differ significantly; if they do not, the r to z formula is used to determine whether or not correlations are significantly different, due to a difference in variance about the regression line. Whether a slope or a variance difference is indicated by these results, it is interpreted as indicative of a difference in the interrelationships of specified variables for differing age groups: in the former case the relationship between variables indicates different slopes for different age groups; in the latter case the relationship between variables is a tighter one for one of the age groups that are being compared.

Regression As an Interaction Detector. Standard multiple regression assesses the relationship between a single dependent variable and two or more independent variables. Let's take the example from the preceding section on correlational analysis, where the correlations between two variables, work affiliation and work interest, were described. The conceptual nature of these variables dictates that work interest is the dependent variable and work affiliation the independent variable; in plain English, finding one's work interesting depends on one's friendly affiliations at work; in statistical language, work affiliation predicts work interest. In the regression analyses performed in this study it is determined initially that one variable be dependent, the other independent, based upon similar, logical assumptions.

However, an additional independent variable, age, is necessary for the present research problem. In this case, age is the state of being middle aged (40 to 49 years) or not middle aged (25 to 39 or 50 to 69 years). The multiple regression formula for the dependent variable, work interest *(Y)*, and the two independent variables, work affiliation *(X)*, and middle-age status *(A)* would be:

$$Y = a + b_1X + b_2A$$

This formula, however, does not assess the *interaction* between age status and the independent variable, work affiliation. It does not inform the researcher whether the relationship between work interest and work affiliation differs depending upon whether or not one is middle aged. In this case, an interaction term is added as a third independent variable; it is derived from the multiplication of the value of the age variable by the value of the work affiliation variable, thus:

$$Y = a + b_1X + b_2A + b_3XA$$

In this formula, the age variable (A) is a dummy variable. Its numerical value indicates whether the variable case is middle aged $(A = 1)$ or not middle aged $(A = 0)$. Given this coding system, when $A = 0$, the regression formula becomes:

$$Y = a + b_1X$$

When $A = 1$, the regression formula becomes:

$$Y = (a + b_2) + (b_1 + b_3)X$$

Given the dummy variable coding, therefore, b_2 signifies the differences between the intercepts, and, most importantly, b_3 signifies the differences between the *slopes* for the groups under comparison (Allison, 1977).

Similarly, the regression formula can be extended so that the dummy variable of age accounts not only for the presence or absence of middle-age status, but for the presence of one of three age conditions: young (25 to 39 years), middle-aged (40 to 49 years), and old (50 to 69 years). This process, too, is based on a coding system of the values 0 and 1. The resulting calculations in turn assess separately whether the slopes are different for the young and middle aged and whether they differ for the middle aged and old.

For the purposes of this investigation, both the two-group age variable (that is, middle aged and nonmiddle aged) and three-group variable (that is, young, middle aged, and old) regression techniques are used, in order to determine whether middle-aged adults differ significantly from either the young, old, or both combined, when examining the interrelationships among variables within the realms of well-being, work, family, and social relationships.

The Structure of Results

The analysis strategy outlined within this chapter lends itself to a clearly defined system for presenting the research results. The four chapters that follow discuss the results within a similar format; dealing in turn with one of each of the four specific domains of life at middle age, namely, the ''quality of life experience,'' ''work,'' ''family,'' and ''social relationships.''

Each chapter begins with a description of the variables that are chosen for examination, followed by a section reporting the results of the initial descriptive techniques: ANOVA, time series plots, and contingency table analysis. The sections thereafter report the results of the correlation and regression techniques. Thus, the variables described initially in terms of age-group difference now are analyzed in terms of the correlations they display differentially at middle age; that is to say, variables now are examined specifically to find out whether their interrelationships differ for men in their 40s. In the case of well-being (within Chapter Three, on quality of life experience), only the intercorrelations among the well-being variables are examined, since they are the most amenable to correlation and regression techniques, from among the variables in Chapter Three. In the cases of Chapters Four, Five, and Six, on work, family, and social relationships, respectively, the intercorrelations among the variables of each of these life domains are reported among themselves and for their correlations with the variables of well-being. Needless to say, for all analyses, the differences and similarities among college and non-college educated men are examined and described.

Hence, by means of the analyses that follow, the reader is informed not only about the general quality of life, the work experience, and the family and social relationships of men in transition to middle age, but also about the unique contributions each of these life domains has to offer to the well-being of men in their 40s.

3
Quality of Life Experience at Middle Age

This chapter probes the general quality of life experience of men at middle age as compared to younger and older men. Quality of life experience, as defined in this analysis, includes an assessment of well-being, of time orientation, and of values, as they change throughout the life span and in particular during the transition to middle age. Subsequent chapters will focus more specifically upon work, family, and social relationships as major domains in the life experience of men. The first section of this chapter describes the measures of general quality of life experience, the next section examines the differences between middle aged men and others on these measures, the third section examines the interrelationships among components of well-being at middle age, and the final section provides a general synthesis of chapter results.

Measures of Quality of Life Experience

The general quality of life experience cannot be assessed by a single measure or even a single approach. Five different types of measures are utilized in the analysis:

1. Internal psychological state
2. Psychological and physical symptoms
3. Sources of life satisfaction
4. Time orientation
5. Value orientation

The first three are measures of well-being. (Appendix A includes the specific items, asked of respondents, that comprise the variable measures; their coded values; and, in the case of composite measures, a list of the items they include.)

Well-Being

Internal Psychological State. Four variables are used to assess the internal psychological state of respondents. The respondents were asked (1) how happy they are and (2) how satisfied they are with their lives. They also were asked to respond to (3) a series of items comprising an index of "zest" (Zung, 1965) and (4) a series of items comprising an index of "self-esteem" (Rosenberg, 1965).

Questions concerning (1) happiness and (2) satisfaction were worded as follows:

1. Taking all things together, how would you say things are these days— would you say you're very happy, pretty happy, or not too happy these days?
2. In general, how satisfying do you find the way you're spending your life these days? Would you call it completely satisfying, pretty satisfying, or not very satisfying?

A score of five on each of these measures indicates that the individual is most happy or satisfied; a score of one indicates he is least.

The "zest" index is based upon the Zung Depression Scale developed in 1965. Because the items of this index were worded in a positive direction, they are more indicative of zest, or lack of depression, than a state of highly depressed affect. There are six items in this index. They ask how often the respondent feels:

1. My mind is as clear as it used to be.
2. I find it easy to do the things I used to do.
3. My life is interesting.
4. I feel that I am useful and needed.
5. My life is pretty full.
6. I feel hopeful about the future.

The highest possible score on this index of zest is 30; the lowest is six. Cronbach's alpha statistic for this measure is .79 for the survey sample of men and .80 for the survey sample of women within the national study.

The "self-esteem" index is based upon Rosenberg's (1965) Self-Esteem

Scale. There are three items in this index. They ask how often the following is true:

1. I feel I am a person of worth, at least as much as others.
2. I am able to do things as well as most other people.
3. On the whole, I feel good about myself.

The highest possible score on this index is 15; the lowest is three. Cronbach's alpha statistic for this measure is .68 for the survey sample of men and .70 for the survey sample of women in the national study.

Symptoms. Four composite indices of symptoms are used in the analysis of middle aged men. These are symptoms of: (1) psychological immobilization, (2) drinking problems, (3) psychological anxiety, and (4) physical ill health.[1] All questions that comprise these four symptom indices were derived by the authors of the original 1957 survey from previous mental-health surveys, with minor rewording on several items (see Gurin et al., 1960) and with the addition of three questions on the use of alcohol and medication unique to the survey in 1976 (see Veroff, Douvan, & Kulka, in press). Respondents answered these questions in a booklet checklist that they filled out themselves (unless unable to read), thereby insuring the privacy of their responses.

The psychological immobilization measure is composed of five items. The items ask how often the respondents have had the following:

1. Do you find it difficult to get up in the morning?
2. Are you ever bothered by nightmares?
3. Do you tend to lose weight when you have something important bothering you?
4. Are you bothered by your hands sweating so that you feel damp and clammy?
5. Have there ever been times when you couldn't take care of things because you just couldn't get going?

A score of 20 represents the highest degree of immobilization; a score of five

---

[1]It should be noted that, although these composite measures are based upon a factor analysis using the sample of men of the present investigation, two of the resulting measures, psychological anxiety and physical ill health, are identical to the symptoms measures derived in the wider study that includes the entire national survey sample of men and women (see Veroff, Douvan, & Kulka, in press). The immobilization measure is also similar to the measure derived from the national sample, except for the inclusion of two additional items and the omission of one other (which is primarily due to the emergence of a "drinking" factor for the sample used in this study).

the lowest. Cronbach's alpha statistic for this measure is .62 for the sample of men and .55 for the sample of women in the national survey.

The drinking problems measure is composed of three items. The items ask how often the respondents have had the following:

1. Do you ever drink more than you should?
2. When you feel worried, tense, or nervous, do you ever drink alcoholic beverages to help you handle things?
3. Have there ever been problems between you and anyone in your family because you drank alcoholic beverages?

A score of 12 indicates a maximal drinking problem; a score of three no problem at all. The alpha statistic for this measure is .67 for the survey sample of men and .62 for the survey sample of women.

The psychological anxiety measure includes five additional symptoms. The items ask how often the respondents have had the following:

1. Do you ever have any trouble getting to sleep or staying asleep?
2. Have you ever been bothered by nervousness, feeling fidgety and tense?
3. Are you ever troubled by headaches or pains in the head?
4. Do you have loss of appetite?
5. How often are you bothered by an upset stomach?

A score of 20 indicates the highest possible psychological anxiety; five the lowest. The alpha statistic for this measure is .69 both for men and women in the national survey.

Finally, the six-item physical-ill-health measure deals exclusively with physical symptoms. Respondents are asked how often:

1. Has any ill health affected the amount of work you do?
2. Have you ever been bothered by shortness of breath when not exercising or working hard?
3. Have you ever been bothered by your heart beating hard?

and to respond "yes" or "no" to:

4. Do you feel you are bothered by all sorts of pains and ailments in different parts of your body?
5. For the most part, do you feel healthy enough to carry out the things you would like to do?

6. Do you have any particular health trouble?

A score of 24 indicates the poorest health; six the best. The alpha statistic for this measure is .77 both for men and for women within the national survey.

In addition to the previous four composite measures, two items about psychological symptoms, unrelated to these measures, are included in the analysis. These questions, which failed to load on the factor dimensions of the preceding four measures, ask about the use of drugs or medicine:

> When you feel worried, tense or nervous, do you ever take medicines or drugs to help you handle things?

They also ask about feelings at some time of an impending nervous breakdown:

> Have you ever felt that you were going to have a nervous breakdown?

A score of four on the question of medication indicates highest usage; a score of one indicates none. The question of a nervous breakdown, on the other hand, is answered either yes (a score of one) or no (a score of two) by the respondent.

Sources of Life Satisfaction. Five questions of identical format were asked of respondents concerning sources of life satisfaction. The questions were introduced to the respondents by acknowledgment of the fact that some people find great satisfaction from some of these things, others none. Specifically, the men were asked to indicate how much satisfaction they themselves got from:

1. Leisure time
2. Work in and around the house
3. Work at a job
4. Being married
5. Being a father

A score of four for each item indicates great satisfaction; a score of one indicates none.

Time Orientation

Two questions were asked of respondents concerning their attitudes toward their past and future:

1. Compared to your life today, how do you think things will be five or
   10 years from now—do you think things will be happier for you than
   they are now, not quite as happy, or what?
2. Compared to your life today, how were things five or six years ago—
   were things happier for you than they are now, not quite as happy, or
   what?

Responses should indicate the degree to which the men are optimistic and the
degree to which they are satisfied at present compared with their past.

Value Orientation

Finally, two questions were asked concerning the values held by respondents.
The men were given a list of nine values:

1. A sense of belonging
2. Excitement
3. Warm relationships with others
4. Self-fulfillment
5. Being well respected
6. Fun and enjoyment in life
7. Security
8. Self-respect
9. A sense of accomplishment

The first question asked:

Which two of these things are most important to you in your life?

The second question asked:

And of these two, which one is most important to you in your life?

Results: Age Differences in Quality of Life Experience

Well-Being

Internal Psychological State. Analysis of variance (ANOVA) results for
the variables of happiness and life satisfaction reveal no significant findings.
Middle-aged men (40 to 49 years) are neither significantly more nor significantly less happy or satisfied with their lives, according to their personal re-

sponses. The result is duplicated in the separate ANOVA tests for both the college- and noncollege-educated men. It should be noted, however, that, among college men, means on happiness and satisfaction are slightly lower among men aged 45 to 49 than men within the other five-year age brackets (with the exception of men aged 60 to 64, who are similarly low).

Results for the composite measures of zest and self-esteem reveal more interesting findings, especially upon stratification by education. The measure of zest reveals middle-age changes for men with college education; the measure of self-esteem reveals middle-age changes for men with a high-school education or less.

Within the college-educated group, in the comparison between men aged 45 to 49 with men of all other ages combined for the measure, zest proves significant $[F(1,208) = 5.7428, p = .017]$. College-educated men aged 45 to 49 are more lacking on the zest measure than men of other ages. These results appear in Table 3.1. Noteworthy, too, is the fact that this same group displays the highest variance on this measure.[2] Figure 3.1 displays these results visually with a time series plot of zest by age, using a moving average of seven. A clear drop in zest occurs among college-educated men during their late 40s.

Results for the self-esteem measure, which appear in Table 3.2, are also significant, but, in this case, for the noncollege-educated men. The ANOVA results for the entire sample of men aged 25 to 69 are significant when grouped in five-year brackets. This result, however, appears to be accounted for by noncollege-educated men. Examination of means reveals lower scores of self-esteem for noncollege-educated men aged 45 to 49 and 60 to 64. It also should be noted that noncollege-educated men in the group aged 45 to 49 display the highest variance on this measure.

In accord with the ANOVA comparisons described in Chapter 2, ideally, noncollege-educated men 45 to 49 should be compared with all others combined (given that means within the combined group do not differ significantly). For the self-esteem variable, however, an exception is made for exploratory purposes of data description. Since men aged 60 to 64 are also low on self-esteem (to the extent they do not significantly differ from men 45 to 49), they are omitted from the comparison. Results, therefore, are significant: men aged 45 to 49 display the lowest self-esteem among men with no college education $[F(1,330) = 5.0483, p = .0253]$. Figure 3.2 displays these results visually with a time series plot of self-esteem by age using a moving average of seven. It is apparent that, until the later years of 60 and beyond, the only noticeable slump in self-esteem among noncollege-educated men occurs during their late 40s.

---

[2]Variances are reported in the tables of this chapter only when they appear to deviate for the age group under scrutiny. When not reported, it can be assumed that variances remain consistent for all age groups being measured.

Table 3.1 Means (and Variances) in Zest*

Age	All[a]		Non-College[b]		College[c]	
	Mean	(Variance)	Mean	(Variance)	Mean	(Variance)
25-29	24.36	(16.47)	24.48	(12.72)	24.55	(18.44)
30-34	24.71	(20.13)	23.69	(19.49)	25.97	(18.58)
35-39	24.53	(16.71)	24.83	(19.02)	24.15	(14.01)
40-44	25.00	(14.81)	24.12	(18.67)	25.91	(9.64)
45-49	23.84	(26.52)	24.41	(18.25)	22.92	(39.91)
50-54	24.81	(23.65)	24.05	(30.65)	25.87	(13.27)
55-59	24.25	(13.83)	24.02	(12.02)	24.40	(16.50)
60-64	22.39	(33.88)	21.91	(36.50)	25.43	(8.29)
65-69	23.09	(30.02)	22.70	(36.14)	24.57	(5.27)

*N values for the differing age groups appear in Table 2.1.

[a]F (8,536) = 1.8337, p = .0648 (n.s.).

[b]F (8,324) = 1.5953, p = .1251 (n.s.).

[c]F (8,201) = 1.4992, p = .1593 (n.s.).

Overall, results on the internal psychological state of respondents indicate differing results for differing measures. Measures of happiness and satisfaction are not highly discriminating. They reveal no significant differences by age. Perhaps a social desirability response tendency prohibits respondents from answering happiness and satisfaction questions in a negative manner. This may be especially so for men, who often feel more inhibited in expressing vulnerability outright (Rosenberg & Farrell, 1976). However, the lack of significant results for these measures may be indicative of a basic continuity in temperament throughout the life span of these men. If, indeed, there is change in their lives, it may be reflected in aspects of well-being other than general happiness or satisfaction, which instead reflect a basic accommodation to life experience.

The composite measures of zest and self-esteem, on the other hand, may be tapping into dimensions of well-being more indicative of a transitional state and reflective of inner assessment. For this reason, perhaps, the more provocative findings appear in the results: college-educated men display less zest during their late 40s; noncollege-educated men display less self-esteem at this point in time. These results are suggestive of a period of inner examination among men during their late 40s, an examination that takes differing forms, dependent upon social background.

The college-educated men at this age lack the zest displayed by others. Perhaps they are diverting their energy toward dealing with internal issues and are resolving on an intrapsychic level the conflicts they perceive in their lives. The noncollege-educated men, at this age, display a loss of self-esteem. It is important to note, in this context, that the items of the self-esteem measure involve a comparison of the self with the qualities displayed by

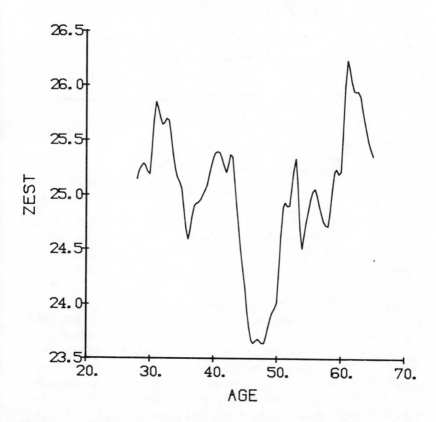

Figure 3.1 Time Series Plot of Zest for College-Educated Men, Based on a Moving Average of Seven.

Table 3.2   Means (and Variances) in Self-Esteem

Age	All[a]		Non-College[b]		College[c]	
	Mean	(Variance)	Mean	(Variance)	Mean	(Variance)
25–29	13.94	(1.75)	13.96	(2.00)	13.94	(1.50)
30–34	13.88	(1.81)	13.68	(1.97)	14.12	(1.56)
35–39	13.59	(3.12)	13.61	(4.01)	13.58	(2.06)
40–44	13.89	(3.16)	13.79	(3.80)	14.00	(2.58)
45–49	13.11	(7.52)	12.56	(8.94)	14.00	(4.17)
50–54	13.76	(1.97)	13.52	(2.46)	14.06	(1.26)
55–59	13.36	(4.05)	13.39	(4.24)	13.44	(3.59)
60–64	12.18	(7.71)	11.80	(7.70)	14.57	(1.29)
65–69	13.79	(1.92)	13.69	(1.90)	14.14	(2.14)

[a] $F_{(8,536)} = 4.8420$, $p = .0001$.

[b] $F_{(8,323)} = 4.7224$, $p = .0001$.

[c] $F_{(8,202)} = .80898$, $p = .5954$ (n.s.).

others. Perhaps, therefore, the noncollege-educated men, during their late 40s, undergo a self-examination stimulated by a social comparison in which they find themselves lacking. Their self-confidence suffers a blow.

Symptoms. Four composite measures are used in the analysis of the symptoms that may trouble men at middle age: psychological immobilization, drinking problems, psychological anxiety, and physical ill health.

ANOVA results for the measure of psychological immobilization for the education groups combined reveals a significant *F* statistic, but show no interpretable pattern of age differences among the five-year groupings of men aged 25 to 69. The reason for this result is evident upon stratifying by education. Noncollege-educated men reveal the highest degree of psychological immobilization at ages 25 to 29; however, college-educated men reveal the highest degree of psychological immobilization at ages 45 to 49. These figures appear in Table 3.3. ANOVA results for the comparison between college-educated men aged 45 to 49 with all others combined are statistically significant [F (1,208) = 4.2170, p = .0413], indicating that college-educated men express more symptoms of psychological immobilization during their late 40s.

A similar pattern of results emerges among the college-educated men for the composite measure of drinking problems, as shown in Table 3.4. The comparison between the college-educated men aged 45 to 49 with all others is statistically significant [F (1,208) = 6.901, p = .0093]. College-educated men admit to more drinking problems in their late 40s than any other age group. They also display the highest variance on this measure.

In contrast to these results, the composite measure of psychological anxi-

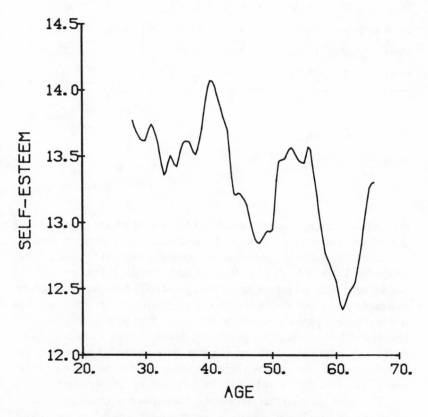

Figure 3.2 Time Series Plot of Self-Esteem for Noncollege-Educated Men, Based on a Moving Average of Seven.

Table 3.3   Means (and Variances) in Psychological Immobilization

Age	All[a]		Non-College[b]		College[c]	
	Mean	(Variance)	Mean	(Variance)	Mean	(Variance)
25–29	7.58	(5.33)	8.05	(6.56)	6.97	(3.16)
30–34	7.42	(6.43)	7.05	(4.00)	7.88	(9.26)
35–39	7.54	(5.32)	7.63	(5.43)	7.42	(5.31)
40–44	6.63	(3.83)	6.67	(4.29)	6.59	(3.47)
45–49	7.29	(4.88)	6.85	(3.29)	8.00	(6.87)
50–54	6.33	(3.31)	6.43	(4.26)	6.20	(2.17)
55–59	6.80	(3.27)	6.78	(3.83)	6.84	(2.47)
60–64	7.17	(7.87)	7.40	(8.65)	5.71	(0.57)
65–69	6.51	(2.14)	6.46	(1.96)	6.71	(3.24)

[a] $F_{(8,537)} = 2.4452$, $p = .0132$.

[b] $F_{(8,327)} = 2.2630$, $p = .0229$.

[c] $F_{(8,201)} = 2.1216$, $p = .0353$.

ety symptoms reveals no significant differences among the age groups, among noncollege-educated men, college-educated men, or both groups combined.

Similarly, results of the composite measure of physical ill health, which appear in Table 3.5, display no noteworthy mean differences between middle-aged men and those older or younger. ANOVA results for the education groups combined and for the noncollege group alone are significant, but this finding is apparently due to the gradual increase with age of physical ill health. ANOVA results on the physical-ill-health measure are nonsignificant for the college sample. Of interest, however, is the relatively high variance displayed by college-educated men aged 40 to 49 on this measure, perhaps indicative of increased awareness by some of symptoms of diminishing health.

The single question that asks whether the respondent uses drugs or medication to help handle tension reveals, again, middle-age differences among men with college education. The comparison between college-educated men aged 40 to 49 and the other age groups combined is highly significant

$[F \ (1,208) \ = \ 6.8514, \ p \ = \ .0095]$. These results appear in Table 3.6. College-educated middle-aged men are significantly more likely to use drugs for worries, nervousness, or tension than men who are either older or younger. They also display the highest variance on this measure.

The final question for analysis concerning symptoms in middle age is the yes/no response to the question of whether the respondent has ever felt he was going to have a nervous breakdown. ANOVA results for the college-educated, noncollege-educated, and both education groups combined are statistically nonsignificant. Age differences within the college-educated group are suggestive, however, of increased awareness of psychological troubles at some point in middle age. Examination of percentages responding yes to this question, which appear in Table 3.7, reveal that a full 20.8 percent of college-educated men aged 45 to 49 years report that indeed they have felt the possibility of a nervous breakdown at some time in their lives. An average of only 12.8 percent of the men at all other ages respond in this manner. (It should be

Table 3.4   Means (and Variances) in Drinking Problems

Age	All[a]		Non–College[b]		College[c]	
	Mean	(Variance)	Mean	(Variance)	Mean	(Variance)
25–29	4.34	(3.25)	4.52	(3.79)	4.09	(2.52)
30–34	3.92	(2.87)	4.19	(4.16)	3.59	(1.16)
35–39	4.04	(2.68)	3.88	(2.68)	4.24	(2.69)
40–44	3.98	(2.55)	3.94	(2.50)	4.03	(2.68)
45–49	4.41	(2.89)	4.10	(2.09)	4.92	(3.91)
50–54	4.14	(2.92)	4.29	(3.51)	3.93	(2.21)
55–59	4.39	(3.69)	4.44	(4.00)	4.32	(3.31)
60–64	3.90	(2.32)	3.80	(2.21)	4.57	(2.95)
65–69	3.66	(2.00)	3.82	(2.37)	3.00	(0.00)

[a] $F \ (8,537) \ = \ 1.2516, \ p \ = \ .2667$ (n.s.).

[b] $F \ (8,327) \ = \ .92945, \ p \ = \ .4921$ (n.s.).

[c] $F \ (8,201) \ = \ 1.8546, \ p \ = \ .0690$ (n.s.).

Table 3.5   Means (and Variances) in Physical Ill Health

Age	All[a]		Non-College[b]		College[c]	
	Mean	(Variance)	Mean	(Variance)	Mean	(Variance)
25-29	10.52	(4.17)	10.66	(5.30)	10.33	(2.73)
30-34	10.61	(4.22)	10.60	(3.42)	10.62	(5.33)
35-39	11.26	(9.42)	11.86	(12.12)	10.49	(5.07)
40-44	11.14	(8.62)	11.42	(7.69)	10.84	(9.68)
45-49	11.48	(10.74)	11.64	(10.29)	11.21	(11.82)
50-54	11.67	(6.06)	11.62	(7.55)	11.73	(4.35)
55-59	12.83	(12.05)	13.56	(14.25)	11.64	(6.49)
60-64	13.85	(17.11)	14.24	(18.28)	11.29	(2.57)
65-69	13.37	(17.83)	13.93	(19.48)	11.14	(6.14)

[a]$F_{(8,537)} = 8.7817$, $p = .0001$.

[b]$F_{(8,327)} = 6.9233$, $p = .0001$.

[c]$F_{(8,201)} = .93089$, $p = .4920$ (n.s.).

noted that although the percentage for college-educated men aged 60 to 64 is also quite high, the N for this age group in the college sample is only seven, rendering the percentages within the cells of the 60 to 64 age group less statistically reliable than those for the age groups with larger sample sizes).

Overall, results derived from the measures of self-reported symptoms reveal highly consistent results among men with more education. On most of these measures, men in their 40s (and especially aged 45 to 49) within the college sample look different from men at other ages, and always in the direction of a greater degree of negative symptoms. Were this group to differ on a single measure only (for example, only on immobilization), one might express reasonable doubt as to whether this was a noteworthy finding; but the consistent pattern observed of college-educated men in their 40s being divergent from other age groups on nearly all measures is quite remarkable, especially given the relatively small size of the sample.

In summary, college-educated men, during their 40s (and in particular, the late 40s), express more symptoms of psychological immobilization, admit to more drinking and use of drugs for tension, show greater variance in self-perception of ill health, and have a somewhat greater tendency to perceive in themselves the possibility of a nervous breakdown at some point in their lives than do the men in the other age groups combined. Certainly, this does not imply that most men with a college education are unduly distressed midway through adulthood. It is important to recognize that they do not display more anxiety symptoms at middle age when compared with other men. Instead, these results suggest some form of internal self-assessment during middle age among the college-educated men. These men lack the zest of men at other ages and are also more immobilized than others at this point in their lives, indicative of an internal focus, as opposed to external action. High variance on the well-being measures similarly may be reflective of an internal focus: responses to questions are more strongly based upon diverging individual proclivities during middle age as compared to the more normative tendencies

Table 3.6 Means (and Variances) in Drug Use

Age	All[a]		Non-College[b]		College[c]	
	Mean	(Variance)	Mean	(Variance)	Mean	(Variance)
25–29	1.17	(.25)	1.09	(.13)	1.27	(.39)
30–34	1.25	(.35)	1.26	(.39)	1.24	(.31)
35–39	1.30	(.53)	1.39	(.72)	1.18	(.28)
40–44	1.35	(.48)	1.27	(.33)	1.44	(.64)
45–49	1.42	(.61)	1.32	(.49)	1.58	(.78)
50–54	1.36	(.41)	1.43	(.56)	1.27	(.21)
55–59	1.38	(.52)	1.42	(.60)	1.32	(.39)
60–64	1.46	(.92)	1.51	(1.03)	1.14	(.14)
65–69	1.44	(.68)	1.52	(.80)	1.14	(.14)

[a] $F_{(8,535)} = 1.1344$, $p = .3381$ (n.s.).

[b] $F_{(8,325)} = 1.3051$, $p = .2399$ (n.s.).

[c] $F_{(8,201)} = 1.0587$, $p = .3937$ (n.s.).

Table 3.7 Percentage Yes Responses within Age Groups to Question of Possible Nervous Breakdown

Age	All	Non-College	College
25-29	14.3%	18.2%	9.1%
30-34	13.2%	14.3%	11.8%
35-39	14.7%	11.9%	18.2%
40-44	10.8%	6.1%	15.6%
45-49	9.5%	2.6%	20.8%
50-54	8.1%	9.5%	6.3%
55-59	10.4%	9.5%	12.0%
60-64	19.2%	17.8%	28.6%
65-69	8.3%	10.3%	0 %

expressed by men of other ages. The examination of the life domains of work, family, and social relations will serve to clarify the content of some of the internal issues relevant to men at middle age, who appear so markedly different from men who are younger or older on well-being measures.

Sources of Life Satisfaction. The contributions of work, family, and social relationships to well-being in middle age are issues that are analyzed in the following chapters via correlation and regression analysis; however, five straightforward questions concerning how much satisfaction is derived from leisure, housework, job, marriage, and parenthood were asked of the respondents. These results are reported in this section, since they ask the respondent directly and in sequence how much satisfaction he gets from these life domains.

Results for the questions concerning satisfaction gained from leisure activities and from work around home display no significant differences among age groups for the entire sample and for the separate education groups.

Results for the question concerning the satisfaction derived from work does provide more interesting results, in particular for noncollege-educated men. These results appear in Table 3.8. ANOVA results for the combined education sample are significant. Stratification by education, however, reveals that this result is due to the characteristics of the noncollege group, where men aged 45 to 49 reveal the highest scores on this measure. The comparison of noncollege-educated men aged 45 to 49 with other age groups combined is statistically significant $[F (1,332) = 6.119, p = .0139]$. Noncollege-educated men in their late 40s derive more satisfaction from their work.

Results of the question asking about satisfaction derived from marriage reveal a marked pattern of transition for men during their 40s. Means for all age groups for this measure appear in Table 3.9. Two comparisons yield significant findings indicative of transition among the combined education sample

Table 3.8   Means in Satisfaction from Work

Age	All[a]	Non-College[b]	College[c]
25–29	3.32	3.23	3.44
30–34	3.45	3.37	3.56
35–39	3.36	3.35	3.36
40–44	3.49	3.36	3.63
45–49	3.65	3.72	3.54
50–54	3.68	3.62	3.75
55–59	3.59	3.61	3.56
60–64	3.49	3.45	3.71
65–69	3.60	3.57	3.71

[a] $F (8,535) = 2.3013, p = .0198.$

[b] $F (8,325) = 2.1183, p = .0337.$

[c] $F (8,201) = .99425, p = .4417$ (n.s.).

Table 3.9   Means in Satisfaction from Marriage

Age	All[a]	Non–College[b]	College[c]
25–29	3.71	3.73	3.70
30–34	3.77	3.78	3.76
35–39	3.81	3.83	3.79
40–44	3.69	3.64	3.75
45–49	3.89	3.92	3.83
50–54	3.80	3.85	3.73
55–59	3.85	3.88	3.80
60–64	3.88	3.86	4.0
65–69	3.91	3.90	4.0

[a] $F\,(8,535)\ =\ 1.9951,\ p\ =\ .0451.$

[b] $F\,(8,325)\ =\ 1.7822,\ p\ =\ .0797$ (n.s.).

[c] $F\,(8,201)\ =\ .64836,\ p\ =\ .7363$ (n.s.).

of men and the noncollege group alone. For both these samples, the comparison between men aged 40 to 44 and the others combined is statistically significant [$F(1,542) = 5.1770, p = .0233$] and [$F(1,332) = 7.3510, p = .007$]. This indicates that men in their early 40s derive less satisfaction from marriage than any other age. Additionally, the comparison between men aged 25 to 44 and 45 to 69 is statistically significant ($F(1,542) = 10.664, p = .0012$] and ($F(1,332) = 9.0622, p = .0028$]. This indicates that at some point during the 40s a transition occurs: men begin to derive significantly more satisfaction from their marriages (starting from an extreme low during the early 40s). These changes are roughly paralleled among college-educated men, but not to a statistically significant extent. The time series plot for this variable, using a moving average of seven, appears in Figure 3.3 and displays these results visually for the combined education sample of men. Readily visible is a slump, followed by a rapid rise during the 40s, in the degree to which satisfaction is derived from the marital relationship.

Results of the question asking about satisfaction derived from parenthood reveal similar findings. Means for all age groups appear in Table 3.10. For the combined education sample and the noncollege group alone, the comparison of men aged 40 to 44 with all others combined is statistically significant [$F (1,543) = 7.0898$, $p = .008$] and [$F (1,332) = 6.6831$, $p = .0102$]. Men in their early 40s derive less satisfaction from the parent role than at any other age. These results also are paralleled roughly by the college-educated sample of men, but not to a statistically significant extent. The time series plot for this variable, using a moving average of seven, appears in Figure 3.4 and displays these results visually for the combined education sample of

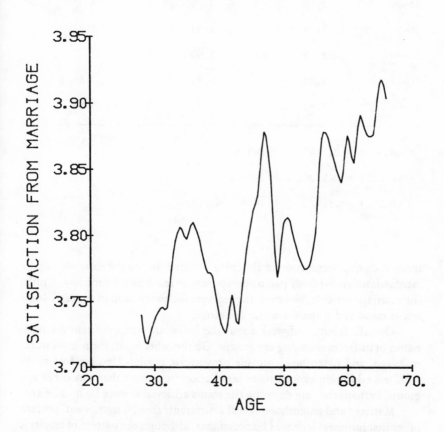

Figure 3.3   Time Series Plot of Satisfaction Derived from Marriage, Based on a Moving Average of Seven.

Table 3.10   Means in Satisfaction from Parenthood

Age	All[a]	Non–College[b]	College[c]
25–29	3.86	3.91	3.79
30–34	3.83	3.88	3.76
35–39	3.74	3.74	3.73
40–44	3.68	3.70	3.66
45–49	3.78	3.79	3.75
50–54	3.89	3.95	3.81
55–59	3.79	3.90	3.60
60–64	3.92	3.93	3.86
65–69	3.91	3.93	3.86

[a] F $(8,536)$ = 2.1247, p = $.0320$.

[b] F $(8,325)$ = 2.1226, p = $.0333$.

[c] F $(8,202)$ = $.54923$, p = $.8183$ (n.s.).

men. A distinct depression in the curve is noted during the early 40s, where satisfaction derived from parenting appears to reach an all-time low. Unlike the marriage variable, however, the recovery following drop in the early 40s is not as rapid and it spans a wider age range.

Overall, leisure and work about the house are nonsignificant discriminators of differences among age groups. On the other hand, the roles of work, marriage, and parenthood provide provocative results. Men aged 45 to 49 with less education express more satisfaction from work than any other age group. Perhaps they are enjoying the status achieved at work by middle age.

Marriage and parenthood reveal a different, though significant, pattern of results; however, it should be noted that, although the pattern of results is similar for college- and noncollege-educated men, the results are statistically of significance primarily for men with less education. While the satisfaction gained from marriage drops during the early 40s, it quickly recovers to a new high by the time the late 40s are reached. Similarly, during the early 40s, satisfaction derived from parenting significantly drops, only to recover gradually through the later adulthood years. Three tentative conclusions are suggested by these results:

1. Patterns of satisfaction during early middle age are similar for parenting and marriage but tend to diverge over time, indicating that these may be separate features of family life with differing affective components.

2. The initial presence of adolescents at home may be especially taxing to men at early middle age, thereby lessening the enjoyment derived

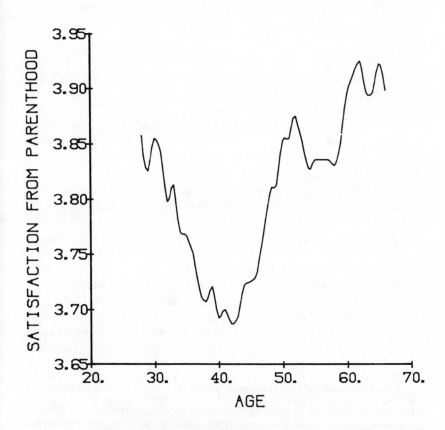

Figure 3.4 Time Series Plot of Satisfaction Derived from Parenthood, Based on a Moving Average of Seven.

from the parent role. (Noteworthy, in this context, is the fact that, by ages 40 to 44, 88 percent of noncollege and 74 percent of college-educated men are confronted first by a child of high-school age.)

3. A renewed interest in the marriage relationship takes place by later middle age. Perhaps the man begins to rely more on his wife as he copes with the problems of middle age, for, as described earlier in this chapter, the middle-aged men do appear to be more highly symptomatic as well as divergent on various measures of general well-being.

The results of the studies by Lowenthal and her colleagues, described in Chapter 1, are relevant to these findings. Their projective measures revealed that middle-aged men perceived more marital than parental themes as they viewed ambiguous pictures, even though both types of responses were equally as likely. These issues are analyzed and discussed further in Chapter 5, Family at Middle Age.

Time Orientation

The men in this study were asked to compare their lives today with their lives five to 10 years from now. Contingency table analysis plots age against the nominal responses of more happy, less happy, or the same. The education groups show similar trends by age: both reveal a transitional pattern during the 40s decade, although they take differing forms. Because men aged above and men aged below the interval 40 to 49 do not differ greatly within, for the purposes of data presentation their categories are collapsed.[3]

Among noncollege-educated men, the contingency table analysis reveals a statistically significant relationship between age and orientation to the future [$\chi^2 (6) = 28.520, p = .0001$]. These results appear in Table 3.11. Readily apparent is the decreased likelihood of expecting the future to be more happy than the present by the age of 40, and the increased likelihood of expecting that it simply will remain the same.

Results on this measure are similarly significant for men with college education [$\chi^2 (6) = 23.975, p = .0003$]. These results appear in Table 3.12. Like the less-educated men, they display a middle-age transition; however, it appears to occur slightly later during the 40s. For, while noncollege-educated men respond more similarly from ages 40 to 49, college-educated men first

_____

[3]It should be noted that for the variable of "future happiness" among noncollege-educated men there is a larger percentage (that is, 33 men or 17 percent) in the older group (aged 50 to 69) for whom responses were not ascertained to this question. Caution should be exercised, therefore, in interpreting actual responses by this group, since a smaller percentage of these men were willing to examine their future happiness, thus presenting a potential bias in responses. Within the college sample, no differential rate of missing cases was noted.

Table 3.11   Percentages within Age Groups of Responses about Future Happiness
for Non-College-Educated Men

Age	More	Same	Less	Total
25–39	64.9%	21.9%	13.2%	100%
40–44	48.3%	45.2%	6.5%	100%
45–49	44.4%	38.9%	16.7%	100%
50–69	31.7%	42.3%	26.0%	100%

experience a shift at age 45, whereupon they become less likely to perceive a happier future and more likely to expect just more of the same (as do the non-college-educated men). It should be noted that there *is* higher pessimism during the 40s for this group, however, as evidenced by the fact that approximately one-quarter of the men in the middle-aged college group expect a less happy future, unlike men older or younger.

The second question concerning the perception of happiness over time asked the men to compare their lives today with their lives five or six years past. Again, contingency table analysis plots age against the nominal responses of more happy, less happy, or the same; and again, a transitional pattern surfaces during the 40s decade, as men 40 to 49 years are compared with men younger (25 to 39) and older (50 to 69). The transitional pattern is revealed when the college and noncollege groups are combined or examined separately; however, they display a somewhat different timing of the transition.

Contingency table analysis for the noncollege group results in a significant relationship between age and orientation to one's past [$\chi^2(6) = 15.066, p = .0198$]. These results appear in Table 3.13. Just as became apparent in the question of future orientation, the largest percentage of men from age 40 onward believe that their past happiness is the *same* as today; hence, it appears that by age 40, among noncollege-educated men, a sense of sameness of past, present, and future becomes more likely. From age 45 onward it also appears that perception of one's past as less happy than today also becomes less likely. In other words, the past is viewed in a less negative light compared to today.

Contingency table analysis for college-educated men also proves significant [$\chi^2(6) = 12.747, p = .0472$]. These results appear in Table 3.14. The increased perception of sameness of past and present (as well as future) also appears for this group, but surfaces not at age 40 as for the noncollege sample,

Table 3.12   Percentages within Age Groups of Responses about Future Happiness
for College-Educated Men

Age	More	Same	Less	Total
25-39	71.0%	23.6%	5.4%	100%
40-44	57.7%	15.4%	26.9%	100%
45-49	38.1%	38.1%	23.8%	100%
50-69	42.6%	46.8%	10.6%	100%

but at age 45. Identical to the noncollege group, however, is the decreased
likelihood of viewing the past as less happy than today.

Overall, results concerning orientation toward future, present, and past
reveal remarkably consistent results for responses by age and education level.
The major difference between the education groups is that the college-educated group experiences most of the shifts at age 45, instead of at age 40. It is
crucial to recognize, however, that viewing one's happiness in past and future
as more happy, less happy, or the same depends upon the state of happiness
the individual feels at the present; therefore, when an individual perceives his
happiness as the same over time, it indicates that he expects no change but it
conveys no information concerning how happy he is at the present.

Table 3.13   Percentages within Age Groups of Responses about Past Happiness for
Non-College-Educated Men

Age	More	Same	Less	Total
25-39	25.7%	28.9%	45.4%	100%
40-44	10.0%	46.7%	43.3%	100%
45-49	27.8%	47.2%	25.0%	100%
50-69	21.6%	47.8%	30.6%	100%

Table 3.14   Percentages within Age Groups of Responses about Past Happiness for College-Educated Men

Age	More	Same	Less	Total
25–39	23.2%	21.0%	55.8%	100%
40–44	21.4%	25.0%	53.6%	100%
45–49	18.2%	50.0%	31.8%	100%
50–69	18.9%	43.4%	37.7%	100%

In summary, men in their 40s begin to perceive a sense of sameness in their lives in past and future happiness. There are fewer great expectations for enhanced happiness in one's future and fewer comparisons of the past and the present where the present clearly is viewed as richer in happiness than had been the recent past. These results mesh well with Bardwick's assumption, discussed in Chapter 1. She asserts that one of the major characteristics of life at middle age is the prevalence of sameness in the self-perception of one's life in retrospect and in prospect, with the conspicuous lack of momentous events that characterize youth and the young-adult years.

Value Orientation

Respondents were asked to choose, from among nine possible values, their two most important. From these two they were asked to choose their first and second most important. Contingency table analysis of the first most important value, plotting the nine values against the nine age groups of the combined sample of college- and noncollege-educated men, is significant. These results appear in Table B1 of Appendix B (p. 138). More significant on a psychological level is the fact that the largest cell in this 9 × 9 matrix occurs for the group aged 45 to 49. A full 33.3 percent of these men choose self-respect as their most important value. This result appears to be primarily due to the college-educated group, however: 45.8 percent of the men aged 45 to 49 choose self-respect as most important. Within the noncollege group, 25.6 percent men aged 45 to 49 choose this value, a lower percentage but nonetheless substantial. Results for the college and noncollege groups appear in Tables B2 and B3 of Appendix B (pp. 139–140).

Within the noncollege group (as appears in Table B2), men aged 40 to 49

choose two value with approximately equal frequency as their most important: security and self-respect (23.6 percent and 23.6 percent, respectively).
The fact that these values are chosen most often by the middle-aged, less-educated men does not differentiate these men too greatly from men at other
ages. Security remains an important value at nearly all ages among the noncollege educated. On the other hand, Table 3.15 shows that, while self-respect
does become a more important major value when compared with men who are
younger, it remains just as important from middle age through later adulthood years for the men in the noncollege group.

Within the college-educated group (as appears in Table B3), self-respect
is more clearly chosen most often as the one most important value for the middle-aged men, and especially for men in their late 40s. No other value is
chosen with comparable frequency. Table 3.15 displays this result in summary form for the self-respect value.

Choice of second most important value results in less uniform findings
and differs for the college and noncollege samples. Tables B4, B5, and B6 in
Appendix B (pp. 141–143) display these results for the combined, noncollege-
educated, and college-educated groups. Among less-educated men aged 40
to 49 years, two values dominate as second most important: warm relationships
with others (22.2 percent) and security (20.8 percent). A higher percentage of
middle-aged men choose these values than the combined percentages of men
older or younger within the noncollege sample.

Within the college-educated sample, results are less consistent for the
middle-aged subgroup. For men 40 to 49, a dominant choice for second most

Table 3.15   Percentages within Age Groups Choosing Self-Respect as First Most Important Value

Age	Non–College	College
25–39	10.9%	22.0%
40–44	21.2%	31.3%
45–49	25.6%	45.8%
50–69	25.9%	31.5%

important value is a sense of accomplishment at 28.6 percent. This result, however, does not differentiate middle-aged men from others. A total of 30 percent of the entire college sample also choose this value. More interesting are the changing results as one moves from early to late 40s. Whereas security is chosen next most frequently (after the value of accomplishment) as second major value (at 21.9 percent) for men aged 40 to 44, only 4.2 percent of men 45 to 49 choose this value. Two other values emerge as dominant choices between ages 45 to 49 and are higher at this age level than the other ages combined: self-fulfillment (29.2 percent) and warm relationships with others (20.8 percent). The percentages of men choosing these values at 40 to 44 years are 9.4 and 6.3, respectively, representing quite an increase in the course of a single decade.

Overall, results on the values measures are suggestive of several themes that characterize the middle-age transition. For all men, self-respect begins to take precedence as a valued goal in life. Ultimately, the self is chosen as the judge of one's own behaviors, attitudes, and accomplishments. Perhaps this is linked to the process of turning inward at middle age that is highlighted so often in the research and theoretical literature described in Chapter 1. In the process, the individual comes to the realization that he is accountable first and foremost to himself; he alone must plan the remainder of his life, and he must make his peace with himself. Self-respect, in this sense, becomes a necessity, a prerequisite to further development and action.

Secondly, the desire for warm relationships begins to emerge as a valued component of living during middle age. This finding blends well with the life-span literature suggestive of renewed affiliative drives among men at middle age. Onset of this value choice appears slightly later for the college-educated men, but its onset, in turn, gives the appearance of a more dramatic rise during the 40s decade.

Finally, education-level differences are highlighted by the results of value selection questions. Among noncollege-educated men, security is continually a dominant concern, placing first and second most important, at all ages. Lowenthal, Thurnher, et al.'s (1975) research on a lower-middle-class sample confirms this finding. The middle-aged men they interviewed were concerned most often with financial matters as they impinged on their families' security at present and for the future.

On the other hand, the college-educated group is less concerned with security, especially past age 44. Accomplishment and self-fulfillment take precedence, accomplishment being important throughout the adulthood years, and self-fulfillment coming into prominence primarily in middle age. Among the more-educated middle-aged men, freed from security worries yet burdened with self-analysis concerns, self-fulfillment provides the logical outlet for tapping into dimensions of the self perhaps stifled in earlier years, due to the driven need to succeed and prosper in young adulthood.

Results: Age Interactions in Measures of Well-Being

Correlation matrices were constructed in order to examine the interrelationships among the well-being variables of happiness; life satisfaction; and the composite measures of zest, self-esteem, immobilization, drinking, psychological anxiety, and ill health[4] for the college group, noncollege group, and both education groups combined. Within these samples, the correlations were calculated for the young (25 to 39 years), old (50 to 69 years), middle-aged (40 to 49 years) and nonmiddle aged (25 to 39, 50 to 69 years) groups. Results indicative of significant age interactions are described in this section.

Significant age interactions among the well-being variables are not abundant, but several do appear in the data, and they do so differentially for the college and noncollege samples.

Psychological Anxiety

Among the college-educated men, psychological anxiety symptoms are intercorrelated more highly with life satisfaction and with zest for men who are middle aged. These results appear in Table 3.16. In other words, among college-educated middle-aged men, as compared with men older or younger, the less satisfied they are with their lives, the more anxious they are; and the more they lack zest, the more anxiety symptoms surface.

These isolated results are difficult to interpret, although they are statistically significant. They may be indicating that different facets of well-being are integrated more strongly for college-educated middle-aged men than for men of other ages, or even men of other educational levels. For this select group it appears that dissatisfaction with life, and lack of zest in general, surface more readily in overt symptoms of anxiety, perhaps revealing a form of internal psychological stress.

Drinking Problems

The correlational analyses reveal an interesting pattern of relationships with the variable measuring drinking problems, a pattern that varies, however, with educational background.

---

[4]Happiness and life satisfaction are included in the age interaction analyses because they are pivotal measures of general well-being. The remaining measures in the analyses of interactions by age are composite indices, since they represent the most reliable and robust measures of well-being.

Table 3.16 Correlations between Psychological Anxiety and Other Well-Being Variables for College-Educated Men

Variables	Middle Aged	Young	Old	Non–Middle Aged
Satisfaction x Anxiety	$-.49^{**}$	$-.23^{*}$	$-.03^{a}$	$-.17^{*a}$
Zest x Anxiety	$-.58^{**}$	$-.29^{*a}$	$-.36^{*}$	$-.31^{**a}$

[*] $p \leq .05$ for correlation coefficient.

[**] $p \leq .001$ for correlation coefficient.

[a] Dummy variable regression comparing age–group slopes indicates a significant ($p \leq .05$) age interaction between the group indicated and the middle aged.

Among noncollege-educated men, drinking problems are related more highly to physical ill health symptoms at middle age than at any other time. These results appear in Table 3.17.

Among college-educated men, drinking is related more highly to psychological immobilization and to self-esteem at middle age than during any other time. These results appear in Table 3.18.

Thus, while self-perception of poor health is related to increased drinking problems among less-educated men, men who are more educated are more prone toward drinking problems if they experience more symptoms of psychological immobilization or if they hold poor self-esteem. Among the noncollege-educated men, perhaps the relationship between drinking and ill health rises in middle age because during this period the man feels more threatened by any indications that his health is in jeopardy, especially within a culture that reveres physical stamina and prowess in men.

On the other hand, among the more educated, physical assets may be less essential to self-esteem, and therefore their loss presents less of an overwhelming threat. Among middle-aged men in this group, struggles with internal issues are more likely to result in turning to alcohol during middle age. Just as the intercorrelations among well-being variables and anxiety symptoms appear more highly related among the men of this group, so also are the well-being variables of immobilization and self-esteem correlated more with problems due to drinking. Again, this perhaps indicates stronger internal integration of well-being components among the more-educated middle-aged men,

Table 3.17 Correlations between Drinking Problems and Physical Ill Health for Non-College-Educated Men

Variables	Middle Aged	Young	Old	Non–Middle Aged
Ill Health x Drinking	.35*	.06[b]	.04[a]	.04[a]

*$p \leq .05$ for correlation coefficient.

[a]Dummy variable regression comparing age group slopes indicates a significant ($p \leq .05$) age interaction between the group indicated and the middle aged.

[b]r to z formula indicates a significant ($p \leq .05$) age difference in strength of relationship in cases where slopes do not differ significantly.

Table 3.18 Correlations between Drinking Problems and Other Well-Being Variables for College-Educated Men

Variables	Middle Aged	Young	Old	Non–Middle Aged
Immobilization x Drinking	.41*	.19	.06	.14[a]
Self-Esteem x Drinking	-.32*	-.04	.05	.00[b]

*$p \leq .05$.

[a]Dummy variable regression comparing age group slopes indicates a significant ($p \leq .05$) age interaction between the group indicated and the middle aged.

[b]r to z formula indicates a significant ($p \leq .05$) age difference in strength of relationship in cases where slopes do not differ significantly.

66

since these well-being intercorrelations peak at this time. Moreover, since immobilization symptoms and drinking problems also peak during middle age for this group (as described earlier in this chapter), a potential problem population is identified at middle age.

Summary of Results

The results of the analysis of the quality of life experience in middle age reveal a number of striking findings that are both consistent with and confirming of the original guiding hypothesis. They are summarized as follows:

1. College-educated men display a number of characteristics during middle age, and especially during their late 40s, that are indicative of possible internal psychological distress when compared with other periods in adulthood. More than men of other ages, they tend to lack zest, express symptoms of psychological immobilization and drinking problems, turn to drugs to relieve nervous tension, display variance in self-perception of ill health, and perceive in themselves the possibility of a nervous breakdown at some point in their lives. Men aged 40 to 49 in the college sample also reveal a greater degree of interrelatedness between different aspects of well-being than do men in other age groups or noncollege-educated men.

It is important, however, not to paint a totally gloomy picture of this stage in life simply by recounting only those findings where more-educated men at middle age respond less positively than others on measures of their well-being. Affectively, they are not at a low; they are not significantly less happy, less satisfied, or more anxious than men of other ages. Most likely, these men have achieved their major goals by this stage in life and therefore they do not despair. On the other hand, the items in which they do respond more negatively, such as lacking zest, feeling immobilized, and turning to drinking and drugs, may be more indicative of internal conflict or immobilizing indecision. This internal state is the likely result of increased introspectiveness at middle age; the inner examination of one's life, accomplishments, and place in society. The task of inner evaluation is not an easy process and likely may prohibit the individual from exerting energies in outward directions until internal issues are scrutinized and resolved in a personally satisfying way.

2. Men with less education display a parallel change in middle age, though not as overwhelming or comprehensive. During the late 40s, men in this group experience a drop in self-esteem as they compare themselves with others. Thus, changes in well-being in middle age appear to occur in a different manner, depending upon social class as defined by educational background.

3. Preliminary descriptive data based upon direct questioning of re-

spondents indicate how much satisfaction middle-aged men derive from differing life domains. According to direct self-reports, noncollege-educated men in their late 40s begin to have increased satisfaction from their work. On the other hand, men in the college and noncollege groups combined begin to view their marriages and parental roles differently at middle age. For both education groups, satisfaction derived from marriage and parenthood plummets by the early 40s; but the life satisfaction gained from marriage begins to peak by the time the men reach their late 40s. These results indicate a developmental difference between the attitudes toward marriage and parenthood during middle age, perhaps as a function of (1) increased turmoil in relationships with teenage and young-adult children and (2) an enhanced appreciation of the long-term relationship with one's wife.

4. Time orientation toward one's own lifespan alters at middle age, regardless of educational level. Men in their 40s begin to perceive a sense of sameness in their lives, as they view their past and project toward their future. Less is expected of the future than in younger days, and the past no longer is viewed as less happy than the present. Perhaps this realization of sameness (be it from a completely happy or a not-too-happy starting point) is triggered by the self-analysis that accompanies the middle-age transition. Perhaps it also is triggered by the realistic realization that no momentous change in one's life can be expected either.

5. Value orientations also transform during middle age. Self-respect begins to take precedence as a most-valued goal in middle age. Ultimately, it is the self to whom one is most accountable, a realization concomitant with the transition to middle age by men in both education groups. As a second-most-valued goal, warm relationships rises to prominence, perhaps indicative of the reemergence of submerged affiliative desires. Other values at middle age differentiate the education groups, however. While less-educated men continue to be concerned with security, more-educated men begin to look for personal self-fulfillment, presumably since worries about material security no longer plague them.

6. Overall results clearly illustrate that men in their 40s are changing on a psychological level and that not all these changes are painless, as displayed by measures of internal state. Several of these changes are similar among men from both educational backgrounds, namely, value orientation, time orientation, and satisfaction derived from family. Other changes appear more dramatic for college-educated men, as indicated by increased psychological symptoms and a drop in zest by late 40s. Perhaps these men truly suffer more. Since practical concerns such as that of security are no longer pressing, they have the luxury of sitting back and evaluating themselves and their lives at the cost of temporary psychological pain. It also may be that men in this group are simply more open and honest, not as fearful of expressing a vulnerability they share with their less-educated counterparts.

4

Work at Middle Age

Any examination of a man's life cycle requires a careful look at his work environment and how he functions within it. This chapter presents results of an analysis of various aspects of work and the work environment among middle-aged men, as compared with men older and younger. The first section describes the measures used in the analysis; the next section discusses the differences between the age groups; the third section analyzes the interrelationships among differing aspects of work; the fourth section describes the interrelationships between well-being and work; and the last section presents a synthesis of chapter results.

Measures of Work

The work environment of the adult involves more than simply the completion of some specified task. Attitudes about and assessment of one's work have several components. Hence, six types of measures are used to examine the place of work in the lives of middle aged men:

1. Job satisfaction
2. Work commitment
3. Perceived job clout
4. Perceived job performance
5. Perceived job relations
6. Motives at work

Appendix A includes the specific survey questions that comprise the variable measures, their coded values, and, in the case of composite measures, a list of the items they include.

Job Satisfaction

A single composite variable is used to measure job satisfaction. This variable includes four different questions, all of which load on a single factor, labeled job satisfaction, at a level greater than .60. The first two questions asked are:

1. Taking into consideration all the things about your job, how satisfied or dissatisfied are you with it?
2. Regardless of how much you like your job, is there any other work you would rather be doing?

The last two ask, "How true is each of your job?"

3. The work is interesting.
4. I am given a chance to do the things I do best.

A score of 16 indicates highest job satisfaction; a score of 4 indicates none. Cronbach's alpha coefficient for this measure is .69 for the survey sample of men and .68 for the survey sample of women in the national study.

Work Commitment

Two separate and different types of variables are used to assess work commitment:

1. If you didn't have to work to make a living, do you think you would work anyway?
2. Taking everything into consideration, how likely is it that you will make a genuine effort to find a new job within the next year?

Job Clout

A single composite variable is used to measure the amount of clout the man perceives he has on the job. It is composed of two separate items that load extremely highly (greater than .80) on a single factor. These questions are:

1. How much does your job allow you to make a lot of decisions on your own?
2. How much say do you have over what happens on your job?

A score of eight indicates optimal clout; a score of two indicates none. The alpha coefficient for this measure is .82 for the survey sample of men and .83 for the survey sample of women in the national study.

Job Performance

A single variable is used to measure the respondent's self-assessment of his job performance. He is asked the straightforward question,

> How good would you say you are at doing this kind of work?

where four indicates "very good" and one, at the opposite pole, indicates "not good at all."

Job Relations

Another single question is used to assess the opportunities available at work for the man to interact with others. He is asked how true the following statement is:

> I am given a lot of chances to talk with the people I work with.

A score of four indicates "very true," and a score of one means "not true at all."

Motives at Work

Two questions are used to derive three measures that assess the degree to which (1) achievement, (2) affiliation, and (3) power are dominant motives at work. The respondent is confronted in both questions with the forced choice between three possible types of jobs:

1. A job where you had to think for yourself (achievement)
2. A job where the people you work with are a nice group (affiliation)
3. A job where you have a lot to say in what's going on (power)

The first question asks which of the three jobs he would like the most; the second question, which he would like the least. He is not informed of the motive (given here in parentheses) each choice signifies.

The responses to these two questions are combined to form an achievement, an affiliation, and a power variable. Each of these three variables is constructed in the same manner. Taking the achievement variable as an example, if on the first question the respondent chooses achievement as most important, this choice is assigned a value of three; any other choices are given a value of one. On the second question, if the respondent assesses achievement as least important, it is assigned a value of one; the other choices each get a value of two. The responses to the two questions are then summed, resulting in a final achievement variable that ranges from two through five, signifying low to high achievement drive at work. It should be noted that these motive questions were asked of only two-thirds of the entire sample of survey respondents; the other one-third were asked different questions not used here.

Results: Age Differences

Job Satisfaction

The job satisfaction measure reveals a consistent pattern of life-cycle change for the college group, the noncollege group, and both education groups combined. At some point between the early and late 40s, job satisfaction dramatically increases and remains at a high level thereafter. Table 4.1 presents the

Table 4.1   Means in Job Satisfaction

Age	All[a]	Non-College[b]	College[c]
25–29	12.23	11.83	12.77
30–34	12.87	12.83	12.91
35–39	12.67	12.79	12.53
40–44	12.82	12.52	13.13
45–49	13.66	13.54	13.83
50–54	13.68	13.55	13.86
55–59	13.70	13.67	13.74
60–64	13.84	13.85	13.83
65–69	14.64	15.00	14.00

[a] $F_{(8,465)} = 4.2234$, $p = .0001$.

[b] $F_{(8,266)} = 3.6650$, $p = .0005$.

[c] $F_{(8,190)} = 1.1673$, $p = .3209$ (n.s.).

means for the separate groups. The comparison of men aged 25 to 44 with men aged 45 to 69 is statistically significant for the college group [$F(1,197)$ = 8.4202, p = .0041], noncollege group [$F(1,273)$ = 20.930, p = .0000], and both education groups combined [$F(1,472)$ = 28.067, p = .0000]. Figure 4.1 displays these results visually for the combined education sample of men, using a time series plot based upon a moving average of seven. Readily apparent is the transitional nature of men during their 40s, for it is during this period that the steepest rise in job satisfaction occurs.

There are two plausible interpretations of this result. First, men during their 40s may become more satisfied with their jobs for several reasons, such as increased seniority and authority as well as the expertise that comes with years of experience. Their salaries also are most likely at their peak, adding to the intrinsic rewards of enjoying the job itself. On the other hand, not all men are likely ever to be *truly* satisfied with their jobs; thus, their 40s probably are the age at which men come to realize the limits to their earlier aspirations and that they may never achieve their dreams of success. Perhaps, therefore, a mechanism of cognitive readjustment takes effect during this stage in life. One may as well be satisfied with the status quo if the alternatives are blocked.

Most probably there are men for whom each of the interpretations is accurate. For successful men in prestigious jobs, the 40s should prove to be a fruitful, productive period in life as applied to the world of work. For the less successful, stifled individuals, there is a need to make do with what they have and come to terms with what they are in the work arena, for only then can they truly feel satisfied with their jobs. Education-group differences that appear in the following section and in the correlation results will bear out these interpretations concerning the correlates of job satisfaction.

Work Commitment

Respondents asked whether they would work if they didn't have to responded either yes, no, or maybe/probably. No significant differences among age groups for the college group, noncollege group, or both education groups combined surface on this measure. Most men, at all ages, would work even if they did not have to. An average of 77.1 percent of the men answer ''yes'' to this question.

Of interest on this measure, however, is the percentage of men answering maybe/probably among the college-educated men aged 45 to 49. A full 18.2 percent of these men answer this question in this ambivalent manner, as opposed to a total of 7.7 percent for the entire college group and 7.9 percent for the total sample. Perhaps this is another symptom of their internal indecision described in the results of Chapter 3. It should be noted, nevertheless, that this group of 18.2 percent, though striking in its response, remains a minority.

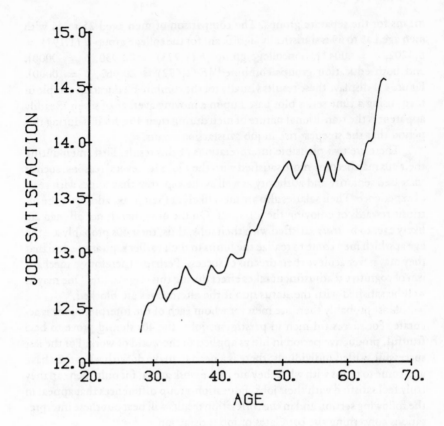

Figure 4.1   Time Series Plot of Job Satisfaction, Based on a Moving Average
of Seven.

Respondents asked about the likelihood of their making an effort to find
a new job within the next year responded either "very likely," "somewhat
likely," or "not at all likely" to this question. Results of the contingency
table analysis for the combined education samples plotting the nine age
groups against the three response categories are significant [$\chi^2 (16) = 29.428$,
$p = .0212$]. Although most men (80.1 percent) state that it is not likely they
will switch jobs, there is a radical increase in this response by the middle 40s.
However, the strength of the combined results appear to be accounted for by
the noncollege group, for whom contingency table analysis proves significant
as well [$\chi^2 (16) = 31.417, p = .0119$). There is no difference found for the
college-educated men.

Results for the noncollege group appear in Table 4.2, where the categories for men aged younger than 40 and older than 49 are collapsed, since they do not differ greatly. Noteworthy is the high expectation of a job switch in the early 40s that is followed by high job stability thereafter. Most likely, men within the lower educational strata find themselves locked into their jobs by their mid 40s, with little chance for change. The early 40s is the age where the man becomes aware that it is his last chance for a break—now or never. Concomitant with the resolution to remain with the same job is the reported increase in job satisfaction described earlier; and greater job stability at the end of the 40s lends support to the interpretation that, once the man realizes his limited work options, he learns to be satisfied with what he has.

The fact that more-educated men display no significant age differences on this measure is also confirmed in the literature on work: men with more education have more job flexibility, even in middle age, unlike their less-educated counterparts, who have less global training and career options in the workplace. Nevertheless, most men in this group report high job stability. An average of 79.8 percent of the college-educated men state that it is unlikely that they will seek out a new job.

Job Clout

The results of the job clout measure are parallel to the results for job satisfaction. There appears to be a steep rise in job clout by the middle 40s, especially for the noncollege sample. Means for each age group appear in Table 4.3. Ac-

Table 4.2 Percentages within Age Groups Reporting Likelihood of Anticipated Job Change for Non-College-Educated Men*

Age	Very Likely	Somewhat Likely	Not Likely	Total
25–39	14.9	14.0	71.1	100%
40–44	23.3	10.0	66.7	100%
45–49	5.7	2.9	91.4	100%
50–69	4.5	2.3	93.2	100%

*χ^2 (6) = 23.966, p = .0005.

cordingly, the comparison between men aged 25 to 44 and men aged 45 to 69 is statistically significant $[F(1,470) = 4.0883, p = .0437]$ for the combined education samples. The separate comparisons for the college and noncollege samples are not significant, although the pattern of means is in the same direction, indicating a midlife transition. Men appear to perceive themselves as having additional clout on the job throughout their 40s, regardless of educational background. Figure 4.2 illustrates this mid-40s transition more vividly by means of a time series plot based on a moving average of seven. According to this graph, where both education groups are combined, the most dramatic rise in clout on the job takes place during the 40s decade.

These results, at first glance, support the supposition that job satisfaction rises during the middle-age transition due to increased authority on the job;

Table 4.3   Means in Job Clout

Age	All[a]	Non-College[b]	College[c]
25–29	6.99	7.10	6.83
30–34	6.95	6.63	7.33
35–39	6.86	6.53	7.25
40–44	6.87	6.35	7.39
45–49	7.26	7.06	7.57
50–54	7.21	6.95	7.57
55–59	7.32	7.24	7.43
60–64	6.84	6.69	7.50
65–69	7.21	7.00	7.60

[a] F (8,463) = .84174, p = .5662 (n.s.).

[b] F (8,266) = 1.1185, p = .3508 (n.s.).

[c] F (8,188) = .92542, p = .4966 (n.s.).

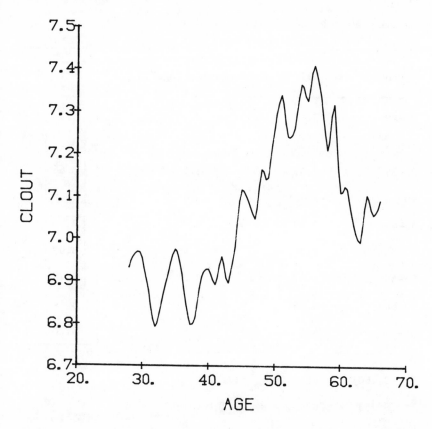

Figure 4.2 Time Series Plot of Job Clout, Based on a Moving Average of Seven.

however, some respondents also may have convinced themselves of their own authority by this stage in the game simply because it is socially expected.

Job Performance

Perceived job performance is assessed by the man's response to the question of how good he thinks he is at his job. Examination of the pattern of mean scores for this variable reveals a middle-age transition for men with college education. These results appear in Table 4.4. Within the college-educated group, men aged 45 to 60 display a substantial rise in self-perceived job performance. The standard comparison between men aged 25 to 44 and 45 to 69 is not tenable, due to the low means of men aged 60 to 69; however, eliminating this group, a comparison between men 25 to 44 and 45 to 59 is indeed statistically

Table 4.4   Means in Job Performance

Age	All[a]	Non-College[b]	College[c]
25-29	3.41	3.33	3.52
30-34	3.32	3.32	3.32
35-39	3.39	3.16	3.66
40-44	3.47	3.45	3.48
45-49	3.43	3.17	3.83
50-54	3.65	3.45	3.93
55-59	3.47	3.25	3.78
60-64	3.28	3.31	3.17
65-69	3.31	3.38	3.20

[a] F (8,460) = .87542, p = .5371 (n.s.).

[b] F (8,263) = .56745, p = .8042 (n.s.).

[c] F (8,188) = 2.9138, p = .0044.

significant [F (1,184) = 13.647, p = .0003], indicative of a middle-age transition toward enhanced self-perception of job performance.

This increase in self-assessed job performance during one's middle age conforms to the expectations of expertise among men of this age range. Their extensive experience and exercise of skills over the years in most cases is likely to have developed their ability to perform their jobs well and efficiently. Neugarten (1968b), correspondingly, has found that well-educated middle-aged adults feel that their judgment is at its best by middle age. This finding is also suggestive of the idea that, among men aged 45 onward, job satisfaction may be related to increased self-perception of good job performance for men with college education, since both performance and satisfaction increase at this time. The correlational analyses that follow will bear out this suggestion.

Job Relations

A rough measure of social interaction on the job is obtained by asking the respondent how often he talks with others at work. The pattern of means indicates that, for both education groups as well as the combined sample, men aged 40 to 49 talk more at work than men of other ages. The means appear in Table 4.5. (Although the mean is highest for college-educated men aged 60 to 64, the N for this age group is quite small, as apparent from Table 2.1). The comparison between men aged 40 to 49 and men of all other ages combined does not quite reach statistical significance [$F(1,471) = 3.3314, p = .0686$] for the combined education sample. This same comparison, done separately for the college and noncollege groups, is similarly nonsignificant; however, for the combined education sample, a comparison between men

Table 4.5   Means in Talking with Others at Work

Age	All[a]	Non-College[b]	College[c]
25–29	3.60	3.50	3.74
30–34	3.65	3.61	3.71
35–39	3.68	3.62	3.75
40–44	3.71	3.65	3.77
45–49	3.76	3.71	3.83
50–54	3.41	3.40	3.43
55–59	3.50	3.33	3.74
60–64	3.66	3.58	4.00
65–69	3.36	3.22	3.60

[a] $F(8,464) = 1.1735, p = .3133$ (n.s.).

[b] $F(8,265) = .91012, p = .5085$ (n.s.).

[c] $F(8,190) = .58913, p = .7861$ (n.s.).

aged 40 to 49 and those 50 to 69 is statistically significant [$F(1,254)$ = 5.5284, p = .0195].

Hence, it appears that there is a small but notable peak in talking with others at work during the transition to middle age among men of all educational backgrounds aged 40 to 49. The content and correlates of talking at work, such as job satisfaction and clout on the job, are analyzed further for their age interactions in the correlation and regression results. It appears, nonetheless, that the social side of work is coming into prominence at middle age.

Motives at Work

Results for the "achievement motive" work variable reveal no significant age differences for either the college group, the noncollege group, or both education groups combined. The "affiliation motive" work variable is similarly nonsignificant for the separate college and noncollege groups; however, there is a significant ANOVA result for this measure when the education samples are combined. It apparently is accounted for by men aged 60 to 64 who display very high affiliation scores; hence, the degree to which achievement or affiliation is considered one's primary motive at work does not differentiate middle-aged men from men of other ages.

Results for the "power" variable prove more relevant for the middle-aged group; they appear in Table 4.6. Examination of means of the combined education groups reveals that men aged 45 to 49 express the strongest motive toward power at work. The comparison between men aged 45 to 49 and the other age groups accordingly is statistically significant [$F(1,317)$ = 5.5124, p = .0195], thus showing that power is a more dominant motive among men at this age.

However, the separate analyses of the two education groups reveals that this result appears to be accounted for primarily by men with college education. Noncollege-educated men aged 45 to 49 display above-average scores on this measure, but the increase is far more dramatic among men with more education. Within the college group, the comparison between men aged 45 to 49 and all others is statistically significant [$F(1,137)$ = 8.7585, p = .0036]; hence, it is primarily men with college education that peak in the drive for power at work during their late 40s.

Noteworthy is the fact that the power motive is signified by the desire for a job where the individual has "a lot to say in what's going on." Not only does this preference imply a desire for power, but it also is suggestive of the exercise of power in interpersonal situations on the job. It is therefore likely that, as more-educated middle-aged men become increasingly sensitive to their status at work, they become increasingly cognizant of the way this status is reflected during their interactions, which also tend to become more frequent at this period of time.

Table 4.6   Means on the Power Motive

Age	All[a]	Non–College[b]	College[c]
25–29	3.42	3.52	3.26
30–34	3.14	2.96	3.35
35–39	3.15	2.89	3.44
40–44	3.00	2.95	3.06
45–49	3.54	3.18	4.19
50–54	3.39	3.17	3.64
55–59	2.84	2.88	2.83
60–64	2.78	2.78	2.80
65–69	2.58	2.53	2.80

[a] $F_{(8,349)} = 2.3825$, $p = .0165$.

[b] $F_{(8,209)} = 1.3186$, $p = .2356$ (n.s.).

[c] $F_{(8,130)} = 1.7705$, $p = .0885$ (n.s.).

Age Differences in Work: A Summary

Several consistent themes are reflected in these results; however, most noteworthy of all are the ever-present indications of transition at middle age, exemplified either by a peak in a score during the middle 40s or by a radical shift in scores from early 40s to late.

For both college- and noncollege-educated groups, the middle-age transition is in evidence in the results of job satisfaction, job clout, and social interaction at work. The source of this change at middle age only can be speculated upon at this point, but it is likely that job satisfaction and clout are expressed by respondents for either one of two reasons: (1) success and status actually have reached a satisfying peak by middle age or (2) at middle age the man becomes resigned to the fact that further advancement is unlikely and therefore needs both to convince himself of current satisfaction and to convince himself and others that he indeed has achieved high status at work. Only at middle age does either of these explanations prove convincing, due to the unique predicament of the middle-aged worker; therefore, it is likely that whichever explanation applies to a particular individual depends on whether the man is truly successful or truly resigned.

The latter explanation may apply especially well to the less-educated worker, who by age 45 becomes locked into his job with little anticipation of any other employment opportunity. The more-educated workers have a wider degree of work options during their middle years, and they also evidence an enhanced assessment of their job performance. Chances are that they do perform at optimal levels during this time and that this sense of competence contributes to their general job satisfaction. The correlational analysis that follows addresses this issue.

Finally, the more-educated men express the strongest motive for power during their late 40s. It is likely that men of this group, sensitive to their status at work, realize that there is greater potential for personal power in interactions with others. Veroff & Veroff (1971) note that, when expectations for power are high, more power behavior is expected. Hence, given that more college-educated, middle-aged men can attain positions of power than can their younger and/or less-educated fellows, the high desire for power at middle age makes considerable sense. It also may be that by middle age power is not sought as an end in itself but is pursued as a vehicle for achievement within the work arena.

Overall, therefore, middle age among college- and noncollege-educated men is a time of change in the work environment. The actual process of working itself may remain either painfully dull or stimulating in content, but the attitudes about what one does and how one expresses oneself on the job change during middle age. This change is in a positive direction, as reflected by the generally more favorable assessments given by these men.

Results: Age Interactions in Measures of Work

Correlation matrices were constructed in order to examine the interrelationships among the work variables of job satisfaction, job clout, job performance, talking with others at work, motives at work, and the variable described in Chapter 3 (on Quality of Life Experience) that measures the amount of satisfaction the individual states he gets from his work. (This latter was one of five variables of quality of life that assessed, more generally, the basic domain of life satisfaction as reflected in self-reports of satisfaction the individuals *de-*

rived from these five realms of experience, on a comparative scale. This differs from the composite job satisfaction variable of this chapter, which measures actual satisfaction with the job.) Matrices were constructed for the college group, noncollege group, and both education groups combined. Within these samples, correlations were calculated for the young (25 to 39 years), old (50 to 69 years), middle aged (40 to 49 years), and nonmiddle aged (25 to 39, 50 to 69 years). Results indicative of significant age interactions are described in this section.

An interesting pattern emerges in the analysis of age interactions. A set of relationships with the variable "job clout" appears uniform for college- and noncollege-educated groups during middle age; however, age interactions among other variables differ for the education samples, especially with regard to the social relations at work.

Job Clout

Correlation and regression analyses show that job clout is integrally related to job relations and job satisfaction during middle age. Table 4.7 illustrates that, during middle age, talking to others is more highly related to job clout than at any other time, and that this relationship nearly disappears by the 50s decade. Similarly, Table 4.8 illustrates that during middle age job satisfaction is more highly related to job clout than any other time and diminishes in importance past the 40s decade. It should be noted, however, that although these relationships are highest at middle age, they do not differ significantly from those for younger men.

The descriptive analysis of the job clout variable in the preceding section of this chapter discusses how, during transition of the 40s, this variable displays its steepest increase for men of all educational backgrounds. It may be that men correspondingly develop a heightened sensitivity to their status at work, which spills over into their social relations and more general job satisfaction. By the 50s, however, enhanced job status is no longer a novelty and therefore no longer may be the major source of job satisfaction or the framework for interactions with one's colleagues at the workplace.

The College-Educated Men:
Job Relations and Affiliation

Among the college-educated men, talking to others is not solely related to the exercise of clout. For men of this group, this variable is related more highly and significantly to job satisfaction and the self-reported satisfaction one gets from work (the latter variable was described in Chapter 3), which are greater during middle age than during any other time. These results appear in Table 4.9.

Table 4.7 Correlations between Job Clout and Talking with Others at Work

Age Group	Non-College	College	All
Middle Aged	.41[**]	.46[**]	.43[**]
Young	.31[**]	.36[**]	.34[**]
Old	.08[a]	.18[a]	.05[a]
Non-Middle Aged	.19[*a]	.17[*]	.20[**a]

[*] $p \leq .05$ for correlation coefficient.

[**] $p \leq .001$ for correlation coefficient.

[a]Dummy variable regression comparing age group slopes indicates a significant ($p \leq .05$) age interaction between the age group indicated and the middle aged (within that column).

Table 4.8 Correlations between Job Clout and Job Satisfaction

Age Group	Non-College	College	All
Middle Aged	.57[**]	.48[*]	.57[**]
Young	.48[**]	.31[*]	.42[**]
Old	.29[*a]	.15	.24[*a]
Non-Middle Aged	.41[**]	.28	.37[**]

[*] $p \leq .05$ for correlation coefficient.

[**] $p \leq .001$ for correlation coefficient.

[a]Dummy variable regression comparing age group slopes indicates a significant ($p \leq .05$) age interaction between the age group indicated and the middle aged (within that column).

A logical explanation for this clear-cut result would be to link both the satisfaction and talking variables with job clout, since both are related significantly to this latter variable and therefore could appear spuriously related to one another. However, a related finding for the talking variable results in the attribution to it of greater explanatory power. This related finding concerns the variable that measures the degree to which affiliation is the most important motive on the job.

Among the college-educated men, the degree to which affiliation is the major motive at work is related more highly and significantly to job satisfaction at middle age than at any other time. This relationship is negative; thus, the degree to which job affiliations are desired is negatively related to job satisfaction. Most important, however, is an assessment of how desire for affiliation is related to actual affiliation. In this respect, correlation and regression show that the motive for affiliation is related more highly, significantly, and also *negatively* to the amount of talking the man does with others at work during middle age than it is at any other time within the college sample. (These results appear in Table 4.10.) It can be concluded reasonably therefore, that

Table 4.9   Correlations between Talking with Others and Work Satisfaction Variables for College-Educated Men

Variables	Middle Aged	Young	Old	Non-Middle Aged
Talking x Job Satisfaction	.64**	.22[b]	.21[b]	.19[a]
Talking x Satisfaction Derived from Work	.60**	.28[*b]	.18[a]	.23[*a]

[*] $p \leq .05$ for correlation coefficient.

[**] $p \leq .001$ for correlation coefficient.

[a] Dummy variable regression comparing age group slopes indicates a significant ($p \leq .05$) age interaction between the group indicated and the middle aged (within that row).

[b] r to z formula indicates a significant ($p \leq .05$) age difference in strength of relationship in cases where slopes do not differ significantly.

Table 4.10   Correlations between the Affiliation Motive and Other Work Variables
for College-Educated Men

Variables	Middle Aged	Young	Old	Non- Middle Aged
Affiliation x Job Satisfaction	-.43[*]	-.03	.08[a]	.00[a]
Affiliation x Talking with Others	-.41[*]	.01[b]	.15[b]	.07[b]

[*] $p \leq .05$.

[a] Dummy variable regression comparing age group slopes indicates a significant ($p \leq .05$) age interaction between the group indicated and the middle aged (within that row).

[b] r to z formula indicates a significant ($p \leq .05$) age difference in strength of relationship in cases where slopes do not differ significantly.

during middle age the absence of interactions with others reduces the amount of satisfaction one has on the job, and the absence of interactions increases the actual desire for interpersonal relations within the work setting.

That this relationship appears only at middle age and only for college-educated men is of interest and leads to several speculations. Perhaps men at this time become more sensitive to their social relations at work and are saddened when they are lacking. They simply want more if they don't have it; and, when they do have it, they are much more pleased with the job. Noteworthy is the finding described in the preceding section of this chapter that men aged 40 to 49 actually do talk more with others at work than men of other ages. Secondly, however, are speculations about the content of these interpersonal relations. Given that these men are middle aged, that many are in bureaucratic middle management, and that they are newly enthralled with senior status, the content of these interactions is likely to reflect this status. During this age, Levinson (1978) stresses the mentor–protégé relationship: at the middle-age transition the man in his 40s transforms from trainee to trainer, and gains satisfaction from guiding the new wave of colleagues. The interpersonal structure of the mentor-protégé relationship provides a perfect format for the exercise of job clout, the sharing of accumulated expertise, and the pleasure of social contact. The shape of the data among college-educated men with regard to social relations at work and satisfaction derived from the workplace supports the supposition that, indeed, men at middle age interact in such a manner.

For this middle-aged group of college-educated men, however, there is another crucial contributor to job satisfaction: competent job performance. Job performance, that is, feeling that one is good at one's work, is related more highly and significantly to job satisfaction at middle age than any other time. (These results appear in Table 4.11.) Hence, the college-educated middle-aged man does not achieve job satisfaction simply by interpersonal means; in order for job satisfaction to flourish, enriched social relations must be complemented by a sense of competent work on the job.

The Noncollege-Educated Men:
Job Clout and a Satisfaction Dilemma

Two results of significance emerge among the noncollege-educated men in the realm of work. Just as, for the college group, affiliative desire is linked with the actual amount of talking one does with others, so it is that, for the noncollege group, affiliative desire is linked with the variable of clout. For this

Table 4.11 Correlations between Job Performance and Job Satisfaction for College-Educated Men

Variables	Middle Aged	Young	Old	Non-Middle Aged
Job Performance x Job Satisfaction	$.59^{**}$	$.04^{b}$	$.04^{a}$	$.05^{a}$

$^{**}p \leq .001.$

[a] Dummy variable regression comparing age group slopes indicates a significant ($p \leq .05$) age interaction between the group indicated and the middle aged.

[b] r to z formula indicates a significant ($p \leq .05$) age difference in strength of relationship in cases where slopes do not differ significantly.

group, job clout is related highly, significantly, and *negatively* to the affiliation motive at middle age only. (These results appear in Table 4.12.) Hence, the more the individual desires affiliation with others at work, the less a sense of personal clout he feels he has on the job. For the less-educated group of middle-aged men, it is most likely that feelings of personal effectiveness (such as having say and making decisions) are exercised in relations with others, whether it amounts to simply talking (a finding that holds true for both education groups) or the actual participation in friendly relations. The men in this group who feel least effective are the ones who feel the need to interact with others the most.

A second puzzling result is found for this group of men: for the middle aged only, there is no relationship found between job satisfaction and self-reported satisfaction derived from work. (These results appear in Table 4.13.) The only plausible explanation for this contradictory result is that middle-aged men with less education are in conflict concerning their work. They may state that their work contributes to their life satisfaction because the response is socially desirable and because the work itself provides financial security essential to their well-being; however, this does not mean that the act of work is satisfying in itself, for by middle age many of these men's dreams of careers have been crushed. They work to derive material support, which is probably at

Table 4.12   Correlations between Job Clout and Affiliation for Non-College-Educated Men

Variables	Middle Aged	Young	Old	Non–Middle Aged
Job Clout x Affiliation	$-.41^{*}$	$-.11$	$.00^{a}$	$-.07^{b}$

$^{*}p \leq .05$.

[a] Dummy variable regression comparing age group slopes indicates a significant ($p \leq .05$) age interaction between the group indicated and the middle aged.

[b] r to z formula indicates a significant ($p \leq .05$) age difference in strength of relationship in cases where slopes do not differ significantly.

Table 4.13 Correlations between Job Satisfaction and Satisfaction Derived from Work for Non-College-Educated Men

Variables	Middle Aged	Young	Old	Non–Middle Aged
Job Satisfaction x Satisfaction Derived from Work	.12	.57[**a]	.48[**b]	.57[**a]

[**] $p \leq .001$.

[a] Dummy variable regression comparing age group slopes indicates a significant ($p \leq .05$) age interaction between the group indicated and the middle aged.

[b] r to z formula indicates a significant ($p \leq .05$) age difference in strength of relationship in cases where slopes do not differ significantly.

a high, but the nature of the work in itself has little to do with satisfaction.

Age Interactions in Work: A Summary

Overall, middle-aged men appear most sensitive to their personal status at work. The clout they exercise on the job is reflected in their patterns of interaction and general job satisfaction. In the more "mellow" 50s and beyond, these relationships no longer hold.

Among more-educated men, the social aspect of work appears to come into prominence as a major contributor to job satisfaction during middle age. Job satisfaction becomes highly related to interpersonal opportunities, and those men who lack these opportunities desire them all the more during their middle age. Noteworthy, too, however, is the fact that middle-aged men with more education also need to feel they are competent at their work, which, along with interpersonal relations, contributes to greater job satisfaction. In light of these results, therefore, it is likely that the mentor-protégé relationship begins to take form at middle age for this group of men.

Among less-educated middle-aged men, more internal conflict becomes apparent. Men in this group appear to need an audience of friendly others in order to display their clout on the job during middle age. Perhaps this provides a sense of assurance of their personal effectiveness. It may be that, while the college-educated middle-aged men perceive affiliative ties as opportunities to exercise power and act as mentors to younger colleagues, the noncollege-educated middle-aged men ascribe less of a power component to affiliation but find that it affords the individual the opportunity to feel effective in the company of his peers.

Most intriguing for the noncollege group is the fact that job satisfaction and self-reported satisfaction from work are unrelated at middle age. Most likely, the financial rewards of their jobs contribute more to life satisfaction than the actual act of working contributes to satisfaction with their jobs.

In general, it appears that multiple factors play a role in job satisfaction during middle age. More than ever, middle-aged men of all backgrounds need to feel effective at their work, to exercise their effectiveness in the company of their coworkers, and to reap the rewards of social relations with subordinates as well as peers.

Results: Age Interactions
Between Work and Well-Being

Correlation matrices were constructed in order to examine the interrelationships among the work variables and the variables that measure well-being. As in the previous section of this chapter, matrices were constructed for middle-aged, young, old, and nonmiddle-aged men who are members of the college group, noncollege group, and both education samples combined. Results indicative of significant age interactions are described in this section.

A fascinating, unexpected result emerges from this analysis concerning the impact of work upon the well-being of middle-aged men. The results indicate that during middle age work satisfaction contributes less to individual well-being than at any other period of life. This occurs among both the college- and noncollege-educated men.

Self-Esteem

A pair of variables illustrative of this result is the well-being variable of self-esteem and the variable described in Chapter 3 that asks the respondent to state how much satisfaction he gets from work. For both college and non-college groups, as well as the groups combined, these two variables are nonrelated during middle age but are related significantly both before and after this stage of life. These results appear in Table 4.14.

It should be noted that regression analysis proves the age interaction to be significant only for the noncollege and not the college sample (although results for this latter group are in the same direction). Most likely, this result is more meaningful for the less-educated men, who, as described in Chapter

Table 4.14   Correlations between Self-Esteem and Satisfaction Derived from Work

Age Group	Non-College	College	All
Middle Aged	.17	-.09	-.02
Young	.29^{*a}	.24*	.26^{**a}
Old	.34^{*a}	.22*	.24^{*a}
Non-Middle Aged	.30^{**a}	.19*	.23^{**a}

$^*p \leq .05$ for correlation coefficient.

$^{**}p \leq .001$ for correlation coefficient.

^{a}Dummy variable regression comparing age group slopes indicates a significant ($p \leq .05$) age interaction between the age group indicated and the middle aged (within that column).

3, plummet in self-esteem at middle age, while they increase in self-reports of satisfaction derived from their jobs. It appears that a positive attitude toward work does not ameliorate poor feelings of self-esteem at middle age. It also may be that self-reports of satisfaction are not fully accurate accounts on the part of these respondents; for, as described in the previous section, the less-educated men display absolutely no relationship between actual work satisfaction and self-reported satisfaction derived from work during middle age.

Life Satisfaction

The life satisfaction variable yields a parallel result to the finding just given. During middle age there is virtually no relationship between life satisfaction and actual job satisfaction for the college group, the noncollege group, or both education groups combined. These results appear in Table 4.15.

Also, as previously stated, this pattern is more clear cut for the noncollege than the college sample. For less-educated men especially, a satisfying job contributes virtually nothing to life satisfaction during middle age, in striking contrast to the self-reports among these men at middle age. Perhaps, indeed, those men who report that their work contributes greatly to their life satisfaction are attempting to resolve an internal conflict concerning their

Table 4.15 Correlations between Life Satisfaction and Job Satisfaction

Age Group	Non-College	College	Age
Middle Aged	-.06	.19	.04
Young	.19[*]	.44[**]	.31[**b]
Old	.27[*a]	.12	.23[*]
Non-Middle Aged	.26[**a]	.35[**]	.29[**b]

[*] $p \leq .05$ for correlation coefficient.

[**] $p \leq .001$ for correlation coefficient.

[a] Dummy variable regression comparing age group slopes indicates a significant ($p \leq .05$) age interaction between the age group indicated and the middle aged (within that column).

[b] r to z formula indicates a significant ($p \leq .05$) age difference in strength of relationship in cases where slopes do not differ significantly.

Table 4.16 Correlations between Zest and Job Satisfaction for College-Educated Men

Variables	Middle Aged	Young	Old	Non-Middle Aged
Zest x Job Satisfaction	.09	.43[**b]	.23	.38[**]

[**] $p \leq .001$.

[b] r to z formula indicates a significant ($p \leq .05$) age difference in strength of relationship in cases where slopes do not differ significantly.

jobs: they *need* to be satisfied with their work, for there is little hope of change in this area of their lives once middle age is reached. Hence, they try their utmost to convince others and themselves of their satisfaction in and from their work, whether or not it exists.

Interestingly, past the 40s, the relationship between life satisfaction and job satisfaction resumes among men in the noncollege group, perhaps as a function of the achievement of a comfortable self-resolution, a decrease in panic, and an increasingly relaxed attitude about oneself and one's work. On the other hand, among the more-educated men past their 40s, life satisfaction remains unrelated to work satisfaction. It is likely that these men find other sources of life satisfaction.

The College-Educated Men: Zest

A final noncorrelate of job satisfaction that occurs only for middle-aged men with a college education is that of zest. Well-educated, middle-aged men who are very satisfied with their jobs nevertheless may lack zest; job satisfaction apparently does nothing to alleviate a state of depression. These results appear in Table 4.16.

Just as self-esteem, which decreases at middle age for the noncollege group, emerges among the less-educated men as unrelated to the job during middle age, so zest, which decreases at middle age for the college-educated group, emerges among the more-educated men as unrelated to the job during middle age. Middle-aged, well-educated men appear to have reached their peaks at work during this period of time. They feel they are most competent then, exercise more power than ever, and rapidly rise in job satisfaction. Nevertheless, they may drop in zest and become dissatisfied with life at this stage, regardless of their status at work. It should be noted that, past middle age for the variable of zest, job satisfaction remains only weakly associated to the well-being of these men.

Overall, it is likely that by middle age, whether successful or not or well-educated or not, men psychologically disengage themselves from the work arena or at least begin to question the value of work in their lives. They participate in job activities and often perform their best in a satisfying way, but work alone at middle age appears not to be enough for a fulfilling, satisfying life, free from the pangs of depression and high in self-esteem.

Summary of Results

In the area of work, once again, men in their 40s appear to represent a group in transition. Several changes take place uniformly among men with college and noncollege backgrounds, but the derivations of these changes seem to differ with educational status. These results and their interpretations are summarized below.

1. Men in their 40s, regardless of educational background, sharply increase in job satisfaction and the clout they exercise on the job. They also tend to do more talking with others at the workplace. What these changes mean, however, differs with social class as defined here by educational background.

Men with less education appear to be more in conflict concerning their work position. Correlation and regression analyses show that the amount of satisfaction they say they derive from work is totally unrelated to job satisfaction during this period of time. At this same point in their lives, they become locked into their jobs; very few anticipate a new job search in forthcoming years. Chances are, therefore, that many of these men become resigned to the status quo, trying to make the best of an unchanging situation that may not be up to previous expectations. Hence they conform their own perceptions of their job satisfaction and job clout to what they think is expected of men their age.

Men with more education appear to fare better at work during middle age. Not only do they have more job clout and more job satisfaction, but they also appear to be closer to positions of power in relations with others. Self-reported competence in work performance also rises at middle age for these men, who still have more options at work than men with less extensive educational backgrounds.

2. Men of all backgrounds also appear more sensitive to their social positions at the workplace during middle age. The more they talk with others, the more they feel they exercise clout and, consequently, the more they gain satisfaction from the job during middle age. Again, however, the dynamics of these relationships differ with education level.

Among men with less education, social relations at work appear to be requisite to the exercise of autonomy in the form of clout. The less clout they report they have, the greater the need for affiliation at work expressed. Apparently, the degree to which they feel they have some say on the job and make their own decisions is related highly to whether they are in the presence of others at work during their middle age.

For men with more education, it appears that the act of talking with others itself may be important regardless of clout. Although men of both groups talk with others more during middle age, if this interchange is lacking among college-educated men, they want it all the more; conversely, when they do talk often with others, they are more satisfied at work. The combination of their enhanced expertise and their desire for social exchange makes it likely that many of these middle-aged men will become mentors to others, thus satisfying the needs for expert performance, sharing with others, and the exercise of their power in the work environment.

3. In spite of the increase in power, prestige, and satisfaction with work during middle age, a surprising change takes place concerning the relationship between well-being and the job. During middle age, analyses indicate that, in comparison especially with earlier adulthood, one's job satisfaction contributes nothing to well-being. Less-educated men drop in self-esteem regardless of the satisfaction they say they derive from work. More-educated men may lack zest in spite of satisfying jobs.

What seems to be occurring at the transition to middle age is a disengagement from work as a source of personal fulfillment, or at minimum a reconsideration of the place work has in one's life. Perhaps this is due to the fact that nearly all that is attainable has been reached by middle age and the challenge of work has diminished. Other sources of fulfillment now must be sought to take its place. On the other hand, it may be that men who are troubled in middle age decide to channel all their energies toward the work they do, only to find that it does not enhance their self-esteem or life satisfaction, or alleviate depression.

A finding suggestive of work disengagement does occur for college-educated men, of whom over 25 percent in their late 40s fail to answer ''yes'' definitively to the question of whether they would work if they didn't have to: eighteen percent of these college-educated men aged 45 to 49 answer this question with ambivalence, stating only that maybe or probably they would work it if weren't essential. The magnitude of this ambivalent response finds no comparison in any other age group.

Overall, however, it is the firm conclusion that, by the transition to middle age, work recedes in importance for the self-fulfillment that comes with a sense of well-being, satisfying as the act of work may be for men of various trades.

5
Family at Middle Age

During middle age, family life is expected to undergo change. Most men aged 40 to 49 have children of high-school age, children who are becoming increasingly independent of their parents. Wives at middle age often are changing themselves as well (Rubin, 1979), as their primary role as caretakers of young children gradually disappears. Family life, as a result, is bound to transform at this time, as middle-aged men begin to cope with a process of internal changes and an altered set of relationships with their children and their wives.

Measures of Family Life

Questions were asked of men in the survey concerning parenthood and marriage. The specific items assessed in this study are described in Appendix A.

Parenthood

A single question is used in this study to assess the individual's self-perception of his adequacy as a parent. Although Chapter 3, "Quality of Life Experience at Middle Age," describes responses to the question of how much life satisfaction is derived from parenting, no question asks directly how happy the respondent is with the role of parent, presumably a question highly subject to a socially desirable response. Less threatening is the question in the present analysis that asks the respondent if he has ever felt he wasn't as good a father as he would have liked, phrased in the following manner:

> Many men feel that they're not as good fathers as they would like to be. Have you ever felt this way?

To this question the respondent was able to answer "yes" or "no."

Marriage

Four questions were asked of the respondent that assess how happy his marriage is and what the quality of his participation in the role of husband is. The first question is straightforward:

> Taking all things together, how would you describe your marriage—would you say your marriage was very happy, a little happier than average, just about average, or not too happy?

A score of four indicates the most marital happiness, and a score of one indicates the least. The man then was probed more specifically about marital problems, with the following carefully phrased question:

> Even in cases where married people are happy, there have often been times in the past when they weren't too happy—when they had problems getting along with each other. Has this ever been true for you?

To this, respondents could answer "yes" or "no."

To assess performance in the husband role, the respondent was asked different types of questions. Parallel to the parental adequacy question just given, the man was asked:

> Many men feel that they're not as good husbands as they would like to be. Have you ever felt this way?

Secondly, he was asked about the relative rewards of the husband role in his particular marriage:

> All in all, who would you say gets more out of being married—you, your wife, or both about equal?

Results: Age Differences

Overall, it appears that these questions asking for self-reports of parenting and marriage do not, for the most part, differentiate middle-aged men from men at other ages, when simply looking at differences by age.

Parenthood

ANOVA comparisons for the variable that measures the yes/no response to whether the respondent has ever felt that he wasn't as good a parent as he would have liked are nonsignificant for the noncollege group, the college group, and both education groups combined.

This result runs contrary to expectations of differences for middle aged men. In light of the increased introspectiveness and consequent self-assessment stressed in the literature about middle-aged men, it would have seemed reasonable to expect that these men would be more willing to admit to their self-doubts as parents. Nevertheless, the data do not bear out this assumption, indicating that self-assessment of parental behavior remains fairly consistent, regardless of one's age or the age of one's children. An interesting difference was present with regard to education: an average of 65.7 percent of college-educated men and an average of 48.2 percent of noncollege-educated men state that they have at some point felt they have not lived up to their expectations as parents.

Marriage

There are no significant differences by age when men are asked to rate the happiness of their marriages. Middle-aged men, on the average, appear to be neither more nor less happy in their marriages than men of other ages, regardless of educational background.

The absence of significant differences when means are compared does not eliminate totally the possibility of change at middle age, for a cross-section of adults of different ages is compared in the analysis, and within-individual change over time is not. As noted in Chapter 1, previous writings about middle age suggest that some marriages improve while others decay; hence, means representing the midpoint between extremes do not necessarily reflect with accuracy the history of the individual marriage and the implications for its current assessment by the middle-aged man. The correlation and regression analyses in the sections that follow, however, will provide more information concerning the relationship between marriage and other aspects of life during middle age.

ANOVA comparisons for the variable that measures the yes/no response to the question of whether the respondent has ever had problems within his marriage are similarly nonsignificant for both of the education samples and the samples combined. Interestingly, however, an examination of the percentages of men answering "yes" to this question are suggestive of increased willingness among college-educated men to admit to marital problems during middle age. College-educated men aged 40 to 49 answer "yes" to this question more often than men younger or older, although the comparison does not quite reach statistical significance [$F(1,203) = 3.4471, p = .0648$]. These results appear in Table 5.1.

It should be noted that a willingness to admit to marital problems does not coincide with lower means of marital happiness among these men. It

Table 5.1   Percentage "Yes" Responses within Age Groups to Question of Marriage
Problems

Age	All	Non-College	College
25-29	71.1%	72.7%	68.8%
30-34	64.5%	61.9%	67.6%
35-39	59.5%	53.5%	67.7%
40-44	67.2%	57.6%	77.4%
45-49	66.7%	56.4%	83.3%
50-54	61.1%	61.9%	60.0%
55-59	60.6%	56.1%	70.8%
60-64	55.8%	55.6%	57.1%
65-69	38.9%	34.5%	57.1%

simply may be that college-educated middle-aged men are more aware of the
flaws in their marriages by virtue of increased self-assessment during this time
in their lives. Levinson (1978) notes that during the transition to middle age,
at about the age of 40, men become more willing not only to scrutinize their
relationships, but to pin the blame upon themselves for problems in their
marriage.

It is important to note, however, the education-group differences for this
question. Just as in the question on parenthood, men with less education are
less willing to admit to possible faults in their marriages. While 70.2 percent
of all college-educated men admit to problems, only 57.3 percent of the noncollege-educated men respond likewise. It may be that the noncollege-educated men are less willing to admit to negative personal assessments, or it may
be that they are less introspective and hence less aware of potential problems
within their close relationships.

ANOVA comparisons for the variable that measures the yes/no response
to whether the respondent has ever felt he was not as good a husband as he
would have liked are similarly nonsignificant for both of the education groups

and the two groups combined. Also, the education-group difference is similar to the other analyses concerning marriage and parenthood. Yes responses to the question of personal inadequacies as husbands were given by 61.4 percent of the college-educated men and 55.5 percent noncollege-educated men.

These results also run contrary to expectations, where the self-analysis of the middle-aged men would be expected to raise the internal question of one's adequacy as a husband in the past or in the present.

Finally, chi-square tests were performed, plotting the variable of age against the nominal responses of self/wife/equal to the question of who gets most from the marriage. Results are not significant for the noncollege sample of men or for the education samples combined; however, results for the college sample are significant, but this appears to be accounted for by the fact that approximately one-quarter (the highest percentage) of men aged 35 to 39 and 55 to 59 respond that they themselves get the most from their marriages. The middle-aged men are not distinctive in the college-educated group.

The general response tendency for this question is that both husband and wife benefit equally from the marriage: 82.9 percent of all college-educated men and 89.2 percent of all noncollege-educated men respond in this manner, representing a small education-group difference.

Overall, results for the questions concerning parenthood and marriage reveal no significant differences among middle-aged men and others. While men with college education admit, in general, to more faults than their less-educated counterparts, the middle-aged men within these groups differ little from those younger or older. The only exception is the suggestive finding concerning marital problems, where more-educated middle-aged men are more willing to confess that problems have occurred.

Results: Age Interactions
in Measures of Family Life

Correlation matrices were constructed in order to examine the interrelationships among the family variables of parental adequacy, marital happiness, marriage problems, and adequacy as a husband. Two measures described in Chapter 3 on the Quality of Life Experience also were used in the analysis: satisfaction derived from parenting and satisfaction derived from marriage. The two education groups, and both education samples combined, were examined for correlations within the young (25 to 39 years), old (50 to 69 years), middle aged (40 to 49 years), and nonmiddle aged (25 to 39, 50 to 69 years).

A single significant age interaction emerges from the analysis of variables of family life. This finding holds consistently for the college group, the noncollege group, and both education groups combined. Specifically, only among middle-aged men are feelings of parental adequacy and adequacy as a husband totally unrelated. At all other ages, these two aspects of self-perception of adequacy in family roles are intertwined significantly. These results appear in Table 5.2.

It appears that middle-aged men, as opposed to men of other ages, differentiate their feelings about parenthood and marriage. If middle age is a period of intensive self-assessment, then perhaps these different aspects of participation in family life are examined carefully by the individual, each aspect on its own, not allowing self-perceived inadequacies in one area of family life to infringe upon the other.

This finding also meshes well with the review of the meager literature concerning family relationships during middle age. In general, it appears that emphasis upon the parental role begins to diminish during the 40s (Clausen, 1976), while sensitivity to the marriage relationship tends to increase in magnitude (Lowenthal, Thurnher, et al., 1975). If, at middle age, the roles of parent and spouse do diverge as sources of personal focus, the finding of their unrelatedness at middle age makes considerable sense.

It is also likely that the parent and spouse roles become reintegrated past middle age, as appears in these results, where the correlations are once again high by age 50 and beyond. Perhaps the individual, once past the middle-age transition, has reestablished these family roles on a new level. With his child,

Table 5.2   Correlations between Parental Adequacy and Adequacy as a Husband

Age Group	All	Non-College	College
Middle Aged	.15	.14	.16
Young	.38[**][a]	.40[**]	.35[**]
Old	.53[**][a]	.51[**][a]	.54[**][a]
Non-Middle Aged	.45[**][a]	.46[**][a]	.41[**]

[**] $p \leq .001$ for correlation coefficient.

[a] Dummy variable regression comparing age group slopes indicates a significant ($p \leq .05$) age interaction between the group indicated and the middle aged (within that column).

he now can relate more genuinely as adult-to-adult; and with his wife he now can relate more genuinely as person-to-person, since both no longer are burdened with the more rigidly defined roles of parents to a young child. More general feelings about human relationships are applied to all family members.

Results: Age Interactions
Between Family and Well-Being

Correlation matrices were constructed in order to examine the interrelationships among the family variables of the preceding section and the well-being variables of happiness, life satisfaction, zest, self-esteem, immobilization, drinking, psychological anxiety, and health. The college group, noncollege group, and the combined education samples were examined for correlation differences among middle-aged, young, old, and nonmiddle-aged groups of men. Results indicative of significant age interactions are discussed in this section.

A single set of results indicating significant age interactions is apparent, which occurs only for men with college education. Specifically, for these men, well-being is related more highly and significantly to marital happiness during middle age than any other time in adulthood. These results appear in Table 5.3. It should be noted that, although the relationships between marital happiness and general happiness and between marital happiness and life satisfaction do not reach significance ($p \le .05$) either by means of regression or r to z calculations, they do behave in the same manner as the variables of zest, self-esteem, and drinking for college-educated middle-aged men. Were the sizes of the age groups larger, significance of differences would be established more clearly for these borderline variable relationships.

These results indicate that the marital relationship is of crucial importance in relation to the well-being of the middle-aged man with college education. This is not to say that these middle-aged men are more happy or less happy with their marriages than men at other ages. What these results may be showing is that, if marriages are less happy than desired, there is a greater threat to the college-educated man's well-being during middle age. Perhaps at this stage of life the man becomes more dependent upon his wife to fulfill his personal needs and to help him to express many of the feelings he has had difficulties showing all his life. The literature on life-span development does suggest an increased sensitivity in men by middle age, a decrease in achievement motives, and an increase in expressive desires. As is apparent from the results of Chapter 4 on Work, moreover, the job environment no longer contributes to the well-being of the middle-aged man. Hence, it stands to

Table 5.3 Correlations between Marital Happiness and Well-Being for College-Educated Men

Variables	Middle Aged	Young	Old	Non–Middle Aged
Marital Happiness x Happiness	.50**	.24*	.19	.22*
Marital Happiness x Life Satisfaction	.46**	.29*	.20	.26*
Marital Happiness x Zest	.37*	.15	−.24[a]	.03[a]
Marital Happiness x Self-Esteem	.56**	.15[a]	.00[a]	.09[a]
Marital Happiness x Drinking	−.38*	−.20*	.21[a]	−.05[a]

*$p \leq .05$ for correlation coefficient.

**$p \leq .001$ for correlation coefficient.

[a]Dummy variable regression comparing age group slopes indicates a significant ($p \leq .05$) age interaction between the group indicated and the middle aged (within that row).

reason that the man turns from work to wife in a search for personal fulfillment and a consequent sense of well-being.

It must be cautioned, however, that these results can be interpreted in the opposite causal direction. It may be that the more unhappy, depressed, and dissatisfied the man feels with himself and with his life, the more vulnerable his marriage becomes to deterioration by middle age. Instead of positing that marital happiness leads to happiness in life, it may be that general personal misery has a greater impact on marriage by middle age. There is no statistical technique that can definitively ascertain the causal direction of this interaction result, given this body of cross-sectional data. Either interpretation, however, leads to a single significant conclusion: the marriage becomes a more crucial component in the lives of these men during middle age, be it that the marriage becomes more capable of enhancing the man's well-being, or be it that the marriage becomes more vulnerable to the man's psychological state.

Summary of Results

The results of the analysis of family life at middle age reveal a number of striking conclusions concerning the middle-age transition. Simply looking at changes by age on single-variable responses proves not as informative as the examination of interaction patterns among the differing components of family life at middle age and among components of family life and psychological well-being. These results and their interpretations are summarized in this section.

1. The examination of family variables for differences by age reveals no outstanding findings. On nearly all measures, middle-aged men respond similarly to those younger and older. Two possible reasons may account for these results. First, most of these questions are highly personal and therefore may be subject to a bias in response; however, this is apparent only upon observation of social-class (as defined here by educational background) differences in responses: less-educated men tend to give more socially desirable responses than more-educated men on measures of this kind. Less-educated men may be more fearful of discussing their vulnerable points, or they simply may be less introspective and therefore may not recognize problematic issues in their lives.

Secondly, and more convincingly, although change is posited at middle age, lack of differences by age in a cross-sectional analysis does not always document accurately intraindividual change by middle age. Also, means and percentages do not convey directly information about those men at the extremes and the sources of their responses. Correlation and regression are more appropriate in this respect, as they explain the reasons why scores may vary while overall means do not differ.

2. A single age difference result, however, does suggest a greater awareness or willingness to admit to marriage problems by middle age, among men with college education. It should be cautioned that this result does not necessarily mean that marital problems increase by middle age; it shows only that an awareness increases concerning the relationship and its problems past and present.

This finding corresponds to much previous theoretical and research work showing that by middle age, most couples first become aware of the nature of their relationship, be it a comfortable one or unhappy, for the interference of young children no longer clouds those issues concerning only husband and wife. The marriage, therefore, can be assessed realistically by both partners. Correspondingly, Clausen (1972) states that by the age of 50 few expect that their spouses will change any further; hence, poor relationships may tend to dissolve while good ones will thrive.

3. In line with the idea of focused marital assessment during middle age is the finding that shows no relationship, in the middle years, between men's appraisals of their effectiveness as parents and as marriage partners. This result corresponds well to the findings discussed in Chapter 3 concerning satisfaction derived from parenthood and marriage. Briefly, men in their early 40s decrease in the amount of life satisfaction they attribute to the roles of father and of husband, but by their late 40s their marital satisfaction increases. It appears, therefore, that attitudes about parenting and marriage begin to run along different tracks by middle age: parenthood recedes into the background as a major focus in life; marriage comes to the forefront as a significant source of life satisfaction.

4. Although these findings are relevant to both educational strata, the significance of the marital relationship is especially prominent, in the present results, concerning college-educated men during their middle age. Only during middle age do marriage and well-being become intricately interrelated for this group of men. The happier the marriage, the more content the college-educated middle-aged man; the more miserable this man, the more unhappy is his marriage.

Regardless of the direction of the causal relationship between general well-being and marriage, the point remains that the marriage becomes an increasingly crucial component of life in middle age. Noteworthy, too, is confirming evidence of this pattern in research by Thurnher (1976), who reports that positive feelings toward one's wife at middle age are highly associated with life satisfaction at this time.

It is important to note, as well, that these results concerning the marriage relationship are especially relevant in light of the results concerning work. It appears there is a trade-off at middle age among college-educated men: while work no longer contributes to the well-being of the man, the marriage rises in importance as a correlate of well-being and as a major focus in life.

6
Social Relationships
at Middle Age

The social relationships of men during their middle age is the least discussed or researched topic in the literature concerning the lives of men; yet, relationships with others are a critical component of the quality of life. For this reason it is important to examine the frequency and impact of social relations at middle age, in order to assess their contributions to well-being during this time of transition.

Measures of Social Relationships

Three areas of questioning comprise the measures of social relations used in the analysis: (1) neighbors, perhaps the most accessible yet superficial form of social exchange; (2) friends and relatives, who can provide an important source of support on a deeper level; and (3) the sense of social connectedness the man feels. The specific items asked of respondents and the questions comprising composite measures appear in Appendix A.

Neighbors

Two variables are used to measure the degree to which the respondent participates in neighborhood ties. The first question asks,

> About how many of your neighbors do you know well enough to visit or call on? Would you say you have many, several, a few, or none?

The second question assesses actual frequency of interaction with neighbors:

> About how often do you visit with any of your neighbors, either at their homes or at your own? Would you say more than once a week, once a week, a few times a month, once a month, or less than once a month?

Friends and Relatives

Four questions are used to measure the extensiveness and quality of relations with relatives and friends. The first question asks straightforwardly about frequency of encounters:

> About how often do you get together with friends and relatives—I mean things like going out together or visiting in each other's homes? Would you say more than once a week, once a week, a few times a month, once a month, or less than once a month?

The next two questions probe deeper than a simple frequency count. The second question asks how many of these relationships the individual can count on:

> Now, think of the friends and relatives you feel free to talk with about your worries and problems or can count on for advice or help—would you say you have many, several, a few, or no such friends or relatives?

The third question asks how often problems actually are discussed with these sources of social support:

> How often, if ever, have you talked with friends or relatives about your problems when you were worried, or asked them for advice or help— very often, often, sometimes, rarely, or never?

Finally, the respondent was asked about actual satisfaction with friends:

> Do you feel you have as many friends as you want, or would you like to have more friends?

Social Connectedness

A single composite measure is used to assess the degree to which the respondent feels a social connectedness with others. The measure includes the following four statements and asks the respondent to assess how true each is for him:

1. No one cares much what happens to me.
2. I often wish that people would listen to me more.
3. I often wish that people liked me more than they do.
4. These days I really don't know who I can count on for help.

A score of 16 indicates the highest degree of social connectedness; a score of four, the lowest. Cronbach's alpha coefficient for the social connectedness index is .67 for the survey sample of men as well as of women, within the national study.

Results: Age Differences

An examination of the measures for detection of differences by age by means of ANOVA comparisons reveals few differences due to age, especially with regard to men aged 40 to 49.

Neighbors

Both the measures that ask about neighbors reveal no significant differences by age for the college group, the noncollege group, or both education samples combined. It appears, therefore, that the number of neighbors the man knows and interacts with has little to do with the age of the man throughout his adulthood years. Perhaps this finding has to do with the man's absence from the home for most of the working day, so that the number of neighbor-neighbor exchanges have no chance to increase in frequency in conjunction simply with changes in age.

Friends and Relatives

Questions that ask about relationships between men and their relatives and friends similarly reveal no differences unique to middle-aged men.

The variable measuring how often the respondent gets together with friends and relatives yields a significant overall ANOVA result, but this result apparently is accounted for by the higher frequency of visiting done by younger men aged 25 to 34 compared to all others. When men aged 25 to 34 are eliminated from the sample, men aged 35 to 69 reveal no differences on this measure. Differences within the two education samples are similarly non-significant.

The variable measuring the number of friends and relatives whom the individual can count on and feel free to discuss his worries with also shows no significant differences within the college sample, the noncollege sample, and both education samples combined.

The variable that measures how often worries actually are discussed with these relatives and friends proves significant for noncollege-educated men and for the combined education group in the overall ANOVA tests; however, this result also apparently is accounted for by the higher scores for younger men aged 25 to 34: men aged 35 to 69 display no significant differences.

Lastly, ANOVA comparisons for the question that asks whether or not the man is satisfied with the number of friends he has also are nonsignificant. Examination of percentages of men answering that they are satisfied reveals that an average of 58.1 percent men (58.5 percent noncollege, 56.9 percent college) state they are satisfied with the number of friends they already have.

Overall, therefore, middle-aged men reveal no unique characteristics in measures of the frequency of their exchanges with others and the quality of these social encounters. Perhaps this is why so little appears in the literature on friendship at middle age, for only the younger men, aged 25 to 34, appear to participate more intensely in relationships with friends and relatives than other age groups.

However, although the frequency of social relations and the talking over of worries with others is not unique to middle-aged men, the impact of these encounters may differ for them, since they do appear qualitatively different from men of other ages on measures of their well-being and the quality of their lives. Correlation and regression, therefore, will assess the impact of social relations through the analysis of statistical age interactions for social relationship variables with variables of well-being.

Social Connectedness

The final composite measure concerning the social relationships of men at middle age, social connectedness, reveals no significant results when comparing age groups by means of ANOVA. Middle-aged men appear to display neither greater nor lesser social connectedness than others.

Of interest on this measure, however, are the variance scores for the noncollege group. Although means do not differ by age for this group of men, the group aged 45 to 49 has nearly double the variance score of men at other ages. While the variance score of men aged 45 to 49 is 9.69, the variance of the other groups combined is 4.99. Hence, while means in the noncollege-educated group display no radical middle-age differences, there appears to be a wider range of extremes of self-perception of social connectedness among these men in their late 40s. The correlates of this variable are explored further in the following sections.

Results: Age Interactions
in Measures of Social Relationships

Correlation matrices were constructed in order to examine the interrelationships among the social relationship variables of neighbors known, neighbors visited, visits with friends and relatives, friends and relatives free to talk with, talking with friends and relatives, satisfaction with friends, and social connectedness. The college sample, the noncollege sample, and both education samples combined were examined for correlations within the young (25 to 39 years), old (50 to 69 years), middle aged (40 to 49 years), and nonmiddle aged (25 to 39, 50 to 69 years).

The comparisons of correlation coefficients of differing age groups reveal no statistically significant differences indicative of age interactions among the social relationship variables. This is in line with the results of no differences among the middle-aged men and others on single-variable measures.

Results: Age Interactions
between Social Relationships and
Well-Being

Correlation matrices were constructed in order to examine the interrelationships among the social relationship variables of the preceding section and the well-being variables of happiness, life satisfaction, zest, self-esteem, immobilization, drinking, psychological anxiety, and health. The college group, the noncollege group, and both education samples combined were examined for correlation differences among middle-aged, young, old, and nonmiddle-aged groups of men. Results indicative of significant age interactions are discussed in this section.

Unlike the results of the investigation of social relationships in and of themselves, an interesting pattern of age interactions appears when social relationships are linked with psychological well-being during middle age. This pattern is especially striking for men with a noncollege background.

The Noncollege-Educated Men:
Contact and Connectedness

Results reveal an intricate pattern of interrelationships between the quality of social contacts and the well-being of noncollege-educated men during their middle age. More so than men at any other age, middle-aged, less-educated men who lack a sense of social connectedness are also most lacking in self-esteem, while those most socially integrated are highest in self-esteem. Secondly, for men of this group, more than men at other ages, those most lacking in zest visit the least with their neighbors, while the most zestful visit with neighbors the most. The final pattern unique to the non-college middle-age group reveals that those who talk over their problems the most with relatives or friends are the men who are most anxious, while those who are least anxious talk over their worries the least. These three correlation patterns appear in Table 6.1.

The fact that these variables in particular are most significant for middle-aged men within the noncollege group corresponds well with previous findings of the present investigation and with other information about the lower- and working-class strata of society (see, for example, Rubin, 1976).

Specifically, the highest correlation that appears in Table 6.1 is that

Table 6.1   Correlations between Social Relationship and Well-Being Variables for Non-College-Educated Men

Variables	Middle Aged	Young	Old	Non-Middle Aged
Connectedness x Self-Esteem	.54**	.15[a]	.27*[b]	.19*[a]
Visiting Neighbors x Zest	.33*	-.04[a]	-.06[a]	-.03[a]
Talking with Friends/Relatives x Psychological Anxiety	.37*	.19	.01[b]	.07[b]

*$p \leq .05$.

**$p \leq .001$.

[a] Dummy variable regression comparing age group slopes indicates a significant ($p \leq .05$) age interaction between the age group indicated and the middle aged (within that row).

[b] r to z formula indicates a significant ($p \leq .05$) age difference in strength of relationship in cases where slopes do not differ significantly.

between self-esteem and social connectedness. Chapters 3 and 4 have shown that, while self-esteem drops during the 40s among men of the noncollege group, work does nothing during this age to bolster slacking self-esteem. Yet, while self-esteem is enhanced in the context of good marital relations among college-educated middle-aged men (as shown in Chapter 5), self-esteem is enhanced, in a parallel way, by a firm sense of social connectedness among those who are less educated. Hence, it appears that self-esteem (an especially susceptible personal trait among less-educated middle-aged men) becomes contingent upon, and is reflected within the context of, social relationships. For the well-educated men, this context is marriage; for the less-educated, this context is the sense of social connectedness derived from more general relationships with others (which may or may not include one's spouse).

The differences in correlates of self-esteem between middle-aged men with and without college backgrounds correspond to the social-class literature, which tends to stress the more role-oriented (as opposed to relationship-oriented) attitudes of lower-class adults toward their marriage and their family (Bernstein, 1970; Rubin, 1976). Lower-class, less-educated men by middle age may not focus as heavily on social intimacies derived from the marital partner as do the more-educated classes; rather, they may focus upon a more amorphous sense of social isolation, realizing but not quite knowing why they may lack intimate and self-supporting relationships with others.

Additionally, it is important to recognize the fact that the self-esteem measure is essentially a social comparison measure of one's own qualities in contrast to others'. The fact that self-esteem is so highly related to a sense of social connectedness implies that less-educated men during middle age base their self-estimations upon the estimations of others; when they fail to derive a sense of self-confirmation from their general social encounters, they become especially susceptible to questioning their own worth.

Table 6.1 also shows that less-educated middle-aged men who display a greater sense of well-being also visit more often with neighbors. The finding of the importance of neighbors also meshes well with literature that describes the differences among the classes. Lower- and working-class adults are much more likely to establish the majority of their social relationships within the immediate neighborhood, as opposed to further away (Rosow, 1967; Rubin, 1976). It may be that the middle-aged men who are more depressed in this group tend more often to shy away from casual and congenial visits with neighbors, perhaps because they have become overly occupied with self-concerns. On the other hand, it also may be that the more zestful noncollege-educated men of this age are especially prone to exert their energies in socially directed ways, having renewed their affiliative desires and appreciation of social ties. In either case, the data show that neighboring remains an integral component of life among the less-educated classes; this is reflected in behaviors during middle age.

On the other hand, Table 6.1 shows that middle-aged men in this group who have more anxiety symptoms tend to talk over their worries more often with relatives and friends. Perhaps by middle age, through the process of self-examination, these men come to the personal conclusion that anxieties no longer can be bottled up inside, but need to be discussed with others who can offer social support. More casual neighbors may not serve this special purpose adequately, so the ears of concerned relatives and friends are sought more often.

Results, overall, for the middle-aged men with less education reveal an enhanced sensitivity to general social relationships and feelings of social connectedness. Men of this group appear more willing to reach out to their closer relationships for support when there is a need; yet they suffer more from poor self-esteem the more isolated they feel from others.

The College-Educated Men:
Immobilization and Social Supports

Results for the college-educated sample of men run parallel to the noncollege group, concerning the need to reach out to others. During middle age, those college-educated men who experience more psychological immobilization symptoms tend to talk over their worries more with relatives and/or friends. These results appear in Table 6.2. The fact that those men who feel immobilized make use of their social supports is especially relevant in light of the fact that they peak in immobilization symptoms during their late 40s and that these symptoms appear to suggest the presence of internal conflict (as described in the results of Chapter 3). Apparently, these college-educated men feel during middle age a need to maintain close human contact when immobilized by conflict on a deep psychological level.

In summary, both college- and noncollege-educated men appear during middle age to become more receptive to their need for social supports when confronted with internal stresses and conflicts that threaten their well-being. Men of both groups make more use of relatives and friends within this situation, but it is men with less education who appear most vulnerable to self-deprecation when they feel disconnected from others. Unwilling to focus more exclusively upon the intimacies of the person-to-person relationship that marriage can provide, as do more-educated middle-aged men, less-educated men at middle age require the self-confirmation that comes with a sense of social connectedness, as opposed to isolation. In the former case, self-esteem is enhanced; in the latter case, it declines.

Table 6.2   Correlations between Talking with Friends/Relatives and Psychological
Immobilization for College-Educated Men

Variables	Middle Aged	Young	Old	Non-Middle Aged
Talking with Friends/ Relatives x Immobilization	.31[*]	−.01[a]	−.01[a]	.02[a]

[*] $p \leq .05$.

[a] Dummy variable regression comparing age group slopes indicates a significant ($p \leq .05$) age interaction between the age group indicated and the middle aged.

Summary of Results

An apparent lack of differences by age in the area of social relationships when frequency counts are examined tends to obscure more substantial relations differentiating the middle aged from others, when examining the interconnections between social behaviors and well-being. The results of this chapter illustrate the utility of a research strategy that proceeds beyond simple frequency measures concerning social behaviors and probes the interrelationships among variables that initially appear no different for middle-aged men than for others. These results and their interpretations are summarized in this section.

1. A straightforward comparison of men of different ages does not differentiate middle-aged men from others when examining the numbers of neighbors, friends, and relatives they know and interact with. Perhaps this apparent lack of differences by age accounts for the absence of such developmental information in the psychological life-span literature. On the surface, they appear indistinguishable from other groups of men.

2. The only finding of frequency comparisons that appears to distinguish middle-aged men from others involves the variable of social connectedness for noncollege-educated men. During their late 40s, men of this group display a wider range of variance on this composite measure. In addition, there is a highly significant relationship between self-esteem and

social connectedness for these men and not for others. The less the social connectedness, the lower the self-esteem.

This result is especially striking in light of the results of this study concerning well-being, work, and family, given in Chapters 3, 4, and 5, respectively. Self-esteem hits a low point at middle age for men with less education; yet work, no matter how satisfying, contributes nothing to self-esteem at this age. But while the more-educated men at this age display enhanced self-esteem in the context of happy marriages, the results of this chapter appear to show that less-educated men display higher self-esteem when they feel a more general social connectedness, as opposed to isolation. Perhaps a component of social connectedness is a feeling of closeness with one's wife as well as with others; however, there is no way to ascertain the underlying structure of this subjectively felt connectedness.

3. A second finding of interest for men of the noncollege sample is the significant correlation between visiting with neighbors and zest during middle age. The more zestful middle-aged man visits more often with his neighbors, perhaps spurred on by affiliative zeal, while the more depressed middle-aged man tends to withdraw instead.

The social-class literature indicates that members of less-educated social strata participate in neighboring relations as a major social and leisure activity. The fact that during middle age the less-zestful men neighbor less appears to indicate that the men of this group who are occupied with internal issues tend not to have the energies to participate in friendly, yet more superficial, social relations. It is impossible to ascertain the personal depth of neighbor relations during middle age, but in light of the findings for men of this group (described in point 4 of this summary) concerning more intimate social relations with relatives and friends, it appears that exchanges with individuals who qualify only as neighbors lack the depth of human exchange that closer relationships offer. Hence, middle-aged, less-educated men seem to forgo neighborly relations for those that are more personally supportive when they feel troubled.

4. Both college- and noncollege-educated men troubled by internal conflict and stress reach out to concerned relatives and friends during the middle-age transition. The less-educated do so when they are psychologically anxious; the more-educated do so when they are psychologically immobilized. Perhaps these men come to value, more than when they were younger, the systems of social support available to them. In line with the life-span literature that describes a resurgence of affiliative desires during the middle-age transition are the results of this chapter, which appear to confirm this developmental phenomenon but in highly specific ways.

Among less-educated men, social connectedness becomes a major component of self-esteem during middle age; among the more-educated, the marriage becomes more crucial to self-esteem. Among the less-educated middle-aged men, a greater reliance during times of trouble upon supportive relationships appears to take the place of more superficial exchanges with casual friends next door. For middle-aged men of all educational backgrounds, however, talking with others over worries and for advice becomes more highly related to the emergence of inner conflict or stress. Middle-aged men, more so than others, appear to realize their needs for support and make an active effort to share their midlife troubles with others who care.

7

Men at Middle Age: The Total Picture

The results described in the preceding chapters on the quality of life experience, work, family, and social relationships in the lives of middle-aged men attest to the uniqueness of this period of time in adulthood. Middle-aged men feel, act, and react in a manner different from men at other ages, be they older or younger. No doubt, there are basic continuities in life experience from youth to old age; but men in their 40s are men in transition, shedding the final vestiges of young adulthood and coming to accept a stage in life with responsibilities to significant others, to society, but, ultimately, to themselves. At worst, a sense of resignation is the outcome of this transition, when hopes of breakthrough success clearly come to a halt with the recognition by the middle-aged man that future growth can only come from within. At best, a sense of wisdom begins to thrive at this time of life, a wisdom that comes with perfection of skills, confrontation of life's contradictions, the passing on of well-learned knowledge to upcoming generations, and fulfillment of the human need to affiliate with others.

This concluding chapter synthesizes the results of the preceding chapters by examining how they coalesce in their confirmation of the guiding hypothesis that men in their 40s differ from others as they make their transit to middle age. This chapter discusses the utility of the exploratory method of investigation used in this study, followed by a substantive discussion of the structure of the results and of how the results convey information about development that is both common to men of all backgrounds and divergent depending upon the social class to which one belongs. Finally, implications for further investigations of middle-aged men are described, now that baseline survey results have been established.

The Exploratory Method

The investigation described in this book of the transition to middle age was designed as an exploratory study. A single, loosely defined hypothesis guided the investigation. More stringently defined experimental hypotheses were avoided for two basic reasons: (1) the research literature provides few definitive principles concerning development at middle age, rendering clear-cut hypotheses difficult, if not nearly impossible and (2) much information capable of being extracted from a rich body of survey data would remain untapped if the research strategy did not leave open many avenues of investigation.

Hence, when searching for middle-age changes, significance was tested for descriptive aims by means of ANOVA comparisons, time series plots, and contingency table analysis. The fact that so often middle-aged men proved different on multiple measures from men at all other ages, spanning from young to old, is a startling result. The middle-aged men were especially deviant in measures of well-being, a finding that was explored further in a search for the contributors to and sources of this basic component of internal life.

In turn, the correlation methods utilized in this study proved to be especially fruitful techniques for the detection of differences at middle-age in the relationships between differing variables (for example, age interactions). They established not only that middle-aged men are different, but provided clues as to why they differ from others in the structure of their lives and in the sources of those feelings and actions unique to men of their age.

The use of multiple regression for the detection of age interactions specified whether or not the numerical slopes representative of the variable relationships of differing groups of men were significantly different. Yet, even if slopes did not differ significantly, it was possible to show that variable relationships for differing age groups differed simply due to tighter or looser variance about the regression line by means of the r to z transformation formula. In this way, even if the direction of a relationship were similar for middle-aged men and the nonmiddle-aged, it was possible to prove that the relationship was a significantly stronger, tighter one for men of one of the age groups under comparison. Hence, whether a slope difference, or solely a tighter variance indicative of a stronger relationship, was indicated, the correlation comparison analysis definitely could indicate how and why middle-aged men differ from others in the interrelationships of various aspects of their lives. This technique is useful from a developmental perspective, as well as from an exploratory perspective, when seeking out the answers to why groups differ on a variety of measures.

It should be noted that the use of age as a major predictive variable in the analyses of this study may be especially well suited to a study of men, as opposed to a study of women. Breytspraak (1974) has shown that age is a major predictor of self-concept for men and not women. Neugarten, in much of her scholarly work, stresses as well the fact that men time their lives in accord with the world of work, women in accord with family stage. Both these findings are highly suggestive of a greater age-relatedness of life-span changes for men, but not for women.

The work environment, whether it be a corporate structure or manual-labor enterprise, is far more uniform in its demands upon men of specified ages, while family life can begin quite young or much later for mothers and wives. A woman of age 35 may have an infant to care for, or a rebellious high-school child; demands on her life and her self-perception are colored by these tasks. Yet, men of age 45 are subtly aware of what their future options are within their chosen trades, regardless of how far they've come until this point and how far they would like to go.

Hence, the method of analysis for detecting midlife changes with age is a far more promising method for the study of men than for women. Were a parallel study of women to be undertaken, a wider number of intervening factors would need to be accounted for, such as age of children and employment status, in addition to the variables of education and age examined in this study.

Quality of Life at Middle Age: Internal State and External Influences

The overall results of this exploratory analysis of middle-aged men as compared with others confirm the guiding hypothesis of a qualitative difference in the lives of men in their 40s. The well-being of men during this age appears to take a turn for the worse, but in highly specific ways. Middle-aged men are not uniformly miserable or distressed. They are no less happy or satisfied than men at other ages. Instead, it seems that they embark upon an exploration of their inner selves, weighing the options they have in their lives from past to present to future. The more-educated men appear to lack zest, are more immobilized, and tend to turn more readily to liquor and drugs; all these measures of well-being indicate an internal focus. They suggest a state of inner tension and indecision at the expense, albeit temporary, of outer-directed action. The less-educated, on the other hand, display not as comprehensive a series of setbacks in their well-being. They do decline, however, in their self-esteem at middle age, a facet of well-being highly related to social comparison, thus suggesting that they, too, assess themselves at this time. Their model for comparison, however, is outwardly derived, much to their self-devaluation during middle age.

Men of this age range, supposedly enjoying the peak of life, appear to be concerned especially with self-evaluation. Other factors involved in the assessment of quality of life experience tend to compliment these well-being results. Orientation toward one's life, past and future, shifts at this point in adulthood. The present no longer is viewed as an improvement on the past; more importantly, the future is expected to be no more happy than is life at the present. A sense of sameness (be it happy or sad) begins to pervade the time perspective of the man at middle age. Perhaps this is why Gould (1972) reports that by the age of 50 the present becomes the most important time dimension in life.

Along with these changes comes a shift in values at middle age. Self-respect becomes a major issue for the man at this stage of life, a noteworthy finding in light of the fact that middle-aged men already have fulfilled the dictates of their roles in society. They have worked hard at their jobs and raised their families according to the rules. By middle age, however, they must determine the rules for themselves. In the process, they seek the self-respect resulting from a careful consideration of life's priorities, their personal needs, and their fulfillment of personal satisfaction (as opposed to giving others satisfaction).

One of these personal needs at this time becomes that of affiliation. Warm relationships with others become a major value in life for many. This need is expressed overtly by the men of this sample, not only in response to a question of values, but also in the results of data on work, family, and social relations during middle age. The need for affiliation is fulfilled in differing ways, depending upon educational background.

Work: Satisfaction and Social Position

In the work arena, men in their 40s confront a major transition. They achieve more status on the job and rapidly rise in job satisfaction. The roots of these changes appear to differ, however, with educational background. The less-educated display more internal conflict concerning their work. Their responses reflect a combination of social expectations and their resignation to a status quo that is not expected to improve. They say they are satisfied with their jobs and work status, but the alternatives are few. By middle age they become locked in.

The more-educated men also report rapid increases during middle age in positive attitudes toward work. Yet, paired with satisfaction is power, authority, and expertise, more potent indicators of success than satisfaction alone.

Men of both educational backgrounds, however, respond to questions concerning the job environment in a manner that demonstrates a heightened social sensitivity at middle age. The less-educated require the presence of friendly coworkers in order to feel they have clout. The more-educated are simply more satisfied when they feel they can talk with others at work, although in this context they are capable of exercising their power. It appears that the draw of the world of work during middle age is comprised of other factors than the basic act of performing a job. Human relations, at this stage, add appeal to the work environment.

No matter the appeal of the work environment, however, the most striking finding within the investigation of this life domain is that satisfaction with the job one does makes absolutely no contribution to the psychological well-being of the man at middle age. He may love his job yet remain unhappy with life; hence, successful or not, it appears that the middle-aged man may disengage from the job he does, as a source of personal fulfillment. This process of disengagement from the work arena is most likely subtle, in light of the overt reports by these men of their great satisfaction with work, a satisfaction that comes not only from reaching the peak of one's work career, but also from the interpersonal side of exchanges on the job.

Close Relationships: Wives and Others

Given that the job is no longer a means toward self-fulfillment and life satisfaction for men at middle age, regardless of education level, other domains within day-to-day life are needed to fill the gap. The results of this study indicate parallel findings for the two groups of men with different educational backgrounds. College-educated men express their feelings of personal well-being within the domain of marriage. Noncollege-educated men express their feelings of well-being within the domain of more general social connectedness. Both these domains are representative of affiliative needs. Their expression, however, differs in accord with the cultural experience unique to the educational background of these middle-aged men.

The more-educated strata of adults within society tend more readily to give verbal expression to intimacy needs, so that the marital partnership is based more often upon its relationship value, as opposed to more regimented role prescriptions. The less-educated, on the other hand, perceive their marriages more often in role-related terms and hence find it more difficult to express their affiliative needs in the context of this potentially intimate relationship.

Lowenthal, Thurnher, et al.'s (1975) results for a group of less-educated middle-aged men have shown that affiliative needs in the marital context are expressed only indirectly through the use of projective measures, a measurement technique not used in the present investigation. Nevertheless, results of this study indicate that less-educated middle-aged men display lower scores in self-esteem the less socially connected they feel. This does not directly implicate the marriage relationship as the major source of affiliative needs, but instead points to the fact that these middle-aged men require some sense of social relatedness to bolster self-esteem.

Related results, however, do implicate the marital relationship directly as a major source of well-being for middle-aged men, regardless of educational background. When the respondents are asked how much their marriages contribute to life satisfaction, men in their late 40s begin to show increased satisfaction derived from their marriages.

Also noteworthy, in the context of family, is parental attitude at middle age. By the early 40s, satisfaction reported from parenting drops dramatically and remains low for some time. In addition, feelings of parental inadequacy become totally unrelated to feelings of marital inadequacy in the minds of middle-aged men, at this stage of life and no other. It appears, therefore, that by middle age the focus switches from parenthood to marriage.

Finally, the social sensitivities of middle-aged men are revealed in results that demonstrate their use of close relationships to talk over worries and problems. The less-educated, when anxious, talk over their worries with relatives and friends. The more-educated talk over their problems when feeling immobilized. Both groups, therefore, reach out to others more when there is a need. The image of self-sufficiency and emotional stability, therefore, is given some leeway for human expressiveness at middle age.

The Middle-Age Transition

The results of this study coalesce, piece by piece, to form a picture of life at middle age; added together, they indicate a period of transition. Well-being results represent the first indication that men in their 40s may be experiencing a time of strain in their lives. In a sense, this transitional period of time can be classified as a crisis, if a crisis is defined globally as the management of internal conflict. Yet, internal conflict, asynchrony, is a developmental necessity, required for growth to occur on a psychological level.

The issues of conflict suggested by the results of this study concern the reorganization of priorities in the domains of work, family, and social relationships. The fact that self-respect becomes a major value for many suggests additionally that societal dictates no longer dominate the decisions made by these men. Instead a resolution of needs and activities is internally derived at this time.

Hence, by middle age, work, a major value for men and source of social identity, recedes into the background, despite the fact that success may be high by middle age. The drive toward achievement and material success diminishes by this age. The less educated continue to be concerned with security needs, presumably due to realistic assessments of present and future finance. The more educated, however, appear to be more materially secure or, at least, no longer concern themselves with security as an important value. In either case, both groups of men no longer rely on the act of work to offer self-fulfillment and to enhance their state of well-being.

In this sense, the transition to middle age becomes a time of personal change, insofar as priorities shift from work to family and friends. The more educated reflect these changes within the marital setting; the less educated reflect these changes in their sense of social connectedness. This general shift corresponds well with changes in time orientation: middle-aged men, regardless of class, begin to perceive past and future as the same. If concentration at middle age were upon advancement at work, future hopes would be reflected in more future-directed responses of expectations for improvement. Relationships, on the other hand, are enjoyed from day-to-day, and therefore better correspond to a time orientation more apparently focused upon the present.

The correlation and regression results of this investigation indicate that the time of transition is focused most heavily during the 40s. Relationships between life domains and psychological well-being tend to shift back to baseline, once the 40s decade of life has passed. Certainly this is not to say that men at age 50 compare with those younger who have not undergone middle age. Instead, these results suggest that life after the middle-age transition proceeds along a new plane of adult development. The major issues of personal choices and priorities have been examined and reorganized, and resolution has been achieved in the course of a difficult period of life. Enhanced appreciation of what work, family, and friends have to offer is recognized by this age. Work can be enjoyed in itself, unhampered by driven ambition for promotion and prestige. Family and friends can be recognized for the social supports they can offer, if and when there is a need. In particular, relationships with child and wife can develop on a new level. Both dyadic relations become less role-restrained past middle age. Children are considered as competent adults (especially once they have begun to raise families of their own); and wives no longer need be viewed in the all-encompassing role of mother.

Overall, the results appear to show that men of all backgrounds experience change during middle age. The form of this change differs, however, depending on social class as defined here by educational status. The general direction, however, is similar for men, regardless of education, from the perspective of shifting priorities and values that lead to well-being.

Suggestions for Future Research

This book represents the first comprehensive effort to establish by means of survey data how men during their middle age differ from those older and younger. Although the results are highly suggestive of a qualitative difference in life at middle age, replication of results using other representative national samples is required to confirm these findings. In particular, larger samples of men who are middle aged would offer a much-needed supplement to the results of this study.

More importantly, comparative analyses are necessary in order to determine whether the results of this national survey study of data collected in the year 1976 represent differences due to developmental change with age, or due to a deviant cohort that happened to be middle-aged at this time. A cohort study by Elder & Rockwell (1978), for example, has shown that men born between 1928 and 1929 suffered greater hardships during the Depression than men born between 1920 and 1921, for they experienced the Depression earlier in their lives and for a longer period of time than those who belonged to the older cohort. Differences during adulthood may be reflective of the unique historical settings experienced by successive cohorts over time and throughout their life-span development. It should be cautioned, however, that historical effects are not the only developmental issue, for historical influences have differing impacts upon a particular cohort, depending upon their social class, their sex, ethnicity, and geographic location (Elder, 1977).

Previous research would tend to support the results of a middle-age transition as an expectable developmental phenomenon, since studies as far back as 50 years suggest alterations at middle age (see, for example, Frenkel-Brunswick, 1968, originally published in 1933). However, the presence of middle-age change and the form that this change can take need to be established definitively by means of cohort, time lag, and longitudinal comparisons that supplement the present cross-sectional results (Baltes, 1968; Glenn, 1977; Schaie, 1965).

A cohort study would involve a comparison of members of this particular cohort at different points in time. For example, similar national data collected in 1957 would indicate whether men who were in their 40s in 1976 displayed similar characteristics when they were in their 20s two decades earlier. In the same respect, if similar national data were collected in 1996, it would be informative to investigate the characteristics of this cohort when its members were in their 60s. In this way it could be determined whether the present cohort is simply different or whether it underwent change at middle age common to all adults.

A time-lag study also is needed to determine whether there are adulthood characteristics unique to middle age. A time-lag study involves a comparison of individuals of the same age, but at differing historical times. From this approach, survey data collected in 1957 would be examined for the characteristics of men aged 40–49, in order to determine whether they were similar to men aged 40–49 in 1976.

Finally, a longitudinal study would involve the collection of data from the same sample of men throughout their lives. By holding the individual constant, developmental change could then be measured at different points over time (such as age 20, 40, and 60), in order to determine whether middle age is qualitatively different.

Schaie (1965) has argued that, in order for the researcher to ascertain an accurate picture of development, all three types of research design must be carried out simultaneously. Baltes (1968), however, has countered that, since the information derived from these three methods is overlapping and redundant, only two of the three need be carried out. Nevertheless, the point remains that, for more definitive conclusions concerning developmental processes over time, data collection at more than one point in time is an essential component, be it that overlapping cross-sectional samples are collected at differing points in time (thus allowing for cohort and time lag comparisons) or that sequential longitudinal samples are measured over time (thus allowing for cohort and intra-individual comparisons of development).

The developmental researcher cannot ignore the effects of cohort and history, along with individual change, in the assessment of development, as provocative as results appear in a single cross-sectional study. Is it that men who became middle aged in the 1970s are unique solely because they belong to a cohort born into the Depression? Is it that middle-aged men in the 1970s were reevaluating their lives because this was an era experiencing a rapid sex-role reversal, when middle-aged wives were entering the work arena in record numbers, to the surprise of their middle aged husbands who traditionally won the bread? Is it that middle-aged men in the 1970s looked differently from others because it was simply in vogue to talk of the "male mid-life crisis"? Only by means of measurements over time, be they cross-sectional, longitudinal, or a combination of both, can the effects of cohort and history be identified and quantified for their effects on middle age. Most likely, all three components of cohort, history, and individual development contribute to the structure of the quality of life at middle age.

Lastly, the specific results obtained in this investigation need to be elaborated further by means of more concentrated series of questions concerning the areas covered and more intensive information concerning the middle-aged men. Results of this study, though significant in a statistical sense, need to be supplemented further by a clinical approach. Often in the course of collection of survey interview data, respondents are not as willing to reveal as many private feelings as may be expressed in more intimate settings where rapport has been established between interviewer and respondent. This issue is especially relevant to respondents who are male, because they less often are willing to express to strangers their vulnerable points. Results of this study further indicate the greater hesitance of less-educated men to describe to the survey interviewer problems with work and family, if in fact they do exist. The establishment of clinical rapport may help to overcome these barriers, so that a potential problem population may be better understood, by means not only of the development of clinical rapport, but also through the use of less direct projective measures, which have proved to be so informative in the studies of Lowenthal and her colleagues.

Specific issues that need to be clarified for men at middle age involve a more definitive determination of the direction of causal relationships. Marriage correlates highly with well-being among more-educated men at middle age. Is it that marriages make them happy, or is it that the more unhappy middle-aged men tend to sabotage their marriages? Similarly, the socially isolated, less-educated men have lower self-esteem during their middle age. Is it that social isolation is an insult to self-esteem, or is it that those with lower self-esteem cannot establish human relationships during this stage of life? More intensive clinical interview data are likely to be informative, but, more importantly, data collected at more than one point in time will be even more suggestive of directions of causality. Longitudinal data, for example, can reveal causal directions through the use of cross-lagged panel correlation statistics designs. A study by Kahle et al. (in press), for example, has illustrated that among male adolescents low self-esteem is the cause of interpersonal problems. Hence, research methods that involve measurements of variables over time are essential, not only for investigating developmental trends accounted for by age, cohort, and history, but for making clearer inferences concerning causal relationships throughout the life span.

Overall, the results of this study have established baseline data in a careful examination of the quality of life experience, work, family, and social relationships during middle age. From this basic starting point, future research can proceed in order to determine the generalizability of the results of this initial study, and in order to microanalyze the intricate interrelationships among the various life domains of men in transition to middle age.

Appendixes

VARIABLE MEASURES

VARIABLES	ITEMS	RESPONSE CODES
I. QUALITY OF LIFE EXPERIENCE (Chapter Three):		
Happiness	Taking all things together how would you say things are these days -- would you say you're very happy, pretty happy, or not too happy these days?	1 = not too happy 3 = pretty happy 5 = very happy
Life Satisfaction	In general, how satisfying do you find the way you're spending your life these days? Would you call it completely satisfying, pretty satisfying, or not very satisfying?	1 = not very satisfying 3 = pretty satisfying 5 = completely satisfying
Zest	How often do you feel: a. My mind is as clear as it used to be. b. I find it easy to do the things I used to. c. My life is interesting. d. I feel that I am useful and needed. e. My life is pretty full. f. I feel hopeful about the future.	6 = low zest 30 = high zest (items a-f: 1 = little or none of the time 2 = some of the time 4 = a good part of the time 5 = all or most of the time)

VARIABLES	ITEMS	RESPONSE CODES
QUALITY OF LIFE EXPERIENCE (continued)		
Self Esteem	How often are these true for you: a. I feel that I am a person of worth, at least as much as others. b. I am able to do things as well as most other people. c. On the whole, I feel good about myself.	3 = low self esteem 15 = high self esteem (items a-c: 1 = never true 2 = rarely true 4 = sometimes true 5 = often true)
Psychological Immobilization	How often have you had the following: a. Do you find it difficult to get up in the morning? b. Are you ever bothered by nightmares? c. Do you tend to lose weight when you have something important bothering you? d. Are you troubled by your hands sweating so that you feel damp and clammy? e. Have there ever been times when you couldn't take care of things because you just couldn't get going?	5 = low immobilization 20 = high immobilization (item a: 1 = never 2 = not very much 3 = pretty often 4 = nearly all the time) (items b-e: 1 = never 2 = hardly ever 3 = sometimes 4 = many times)

VARIABLES	ITEMS	RESPONSE CODES
QUALITY OF LIFE EXPERIENCE (continued)		
Drinking Problems	How often have you had the following:	3 = no drinking problem 12 = high drinking problem
	a. Do you ever drink more than you should?	(items a-c: 1 = never 2 = hardly ever 3 = sometimes 4 = many times)
	b. When you feel worried, tense, or nervous, do you ever drink alcoholic beverages to help you handle things?	
	c. Have there ever been problems between you and anyone in your family because you drank alcoholic beverages?	
Psychological Anxiety	How often have you had the following:	5 = low anxiety 20 = high anxiety
	a. Do you ever have any trouble getting to sleep or staying asleep?	(items a-e: 1 = never 2 = not very much 3 = pretty often 4 = nearly all the time)
	b. Have you ever been bothered by nervousness, feeling fidgety and tense?	
	c. Are you ever troubled by headaches or pains in the head?	
	d. Do you have loss of appetite?	
	e. How often are you bothered by having an upset stomach?	

129

VARIABLES	ITEMS	RESPONSE CODES

QUALITY OF LIFE EXPERIENCE (continued)

Physical Ill Health

How often have you had the following (a-c):

a. Has any ill health affected the amount of work you do?

b. Have you ever been bothered by shortness of breath when not exercising or working hard?

c. Have you ever been bothered by your heart beating hard?

Just answer yes or no (d-f):

d. Do you feel you are bothered by all sorts of pains and ailments in different parts of your body?

e. For the most part, do you feel healthy enough to carry out the things you would like to do?

f. Do you have any particular health trouble?

RESPONSE CODES:

6 = good health
24 = poor health

(items a-c:
1 = never
2 = hardly ever
3 = sometimes
4 = many times)

(item d:
2 = no
4 = yes)

(item e:
2 = yes
4 = no)

(item f:
2 = no
4 = yes)

Drug Use

When you feel worried, tense or nervous, do you ever take medicines or drugs to help you handle things?

1 = never
2 = hardly ever
3 = sometimes
4 = many times

130

VARIABLES	ITEMS	RESPONSE CODES

QUALITY OF LIFE EXPERIENCE
(continued)

Nervous Breakdown

Have you ever felt that you were
going to have a nervous breakdown?

1 = yes
2 = no

Sources of Satisfaction

Some things in our lives are very
satisfying to one person, while
another may not find them satisfying at all. I'd like to ask how
much satisfaction you have gotten
from some of these different things:

1. Leisure

a. First, consider the things you
   do in your leisure time.

2. Work in the House

b. How about the work you do in and
   around the house?

3. Work at Job

c. How much satisfaction have you
   gotten from work at a job?

4. Marriage

d. What about being married?

5. Parenthood

e. How much satisfaction have you
   gotten out of being a father?

Items a-e:
1 = no satisfaction
2 = little satisfaction
3 = some satisfaction
4 = great satisfaction

Future Happiness

Compared to your life today, how do
you think things will be 5 or 10
years from now -- do you think
things will be happier for you than
they are now, not quite as happy, or
what?

1 = more
2 = same
3 = less

131

VARIABLES	ITEMS	RESPONSE CODES
QUALITY OF LIFE EXPERIENCE (continued)		
Past Happiness	Compared to your life today, how were things 5 or 6 years ago -- were things happier for you than they are now, not quite as happy, or what?	1 = more 2 = same 3 = less
Values:	Here is a list of things that many people look for or want out of life. Please study the list carefully, then tell me:	Items a-b: 1 = sense of belonging 2 = excitement 3 = warm relationships with others
1. First Most Important Value	a. Which two of these things are most important to you in your life?	4 = self fulfillment 5 = being well respected 6 = fun and enjoyment in life 7 = security
2. Second Most Important Value	b. And of these two, which one is most important to you in your life?	8 = self respect 9 = a sense of accomplishment
II. WORK (Chapter Four):		
Job Satisfaction	a. Taking into consideration all the things about your job, how satisfied or dissatisfied are you with it?	4 = low satisfaction 16 = high satisfaction (Item a: 1 = very unsatisfied; unsatisfied 2 = neutral; ambivalent 3 = satisfied 4 = very satisfied)
	b. Regardless of how much you like your job, is there any other work you'd rather be doing?	(Item b: 2 = yes 4 = no)

VARIABLES	ITEMS	RESPONSE CODES
WORK (continued)		
Job Satisfaction (continued)	Please tell me how true each is of your job (c-d): c. The work is interesting. d. I am given a chance to do the things I do best.	(Items c-d: 1 = not at all true 2 = not very true 3 = somewhat true 4 = very true)
Desire to Work	If you didn't have to work to make a living, do you think you would work anyway?	1 = yes 2 = maybe; probably 3 = no
Finding New Job	Taking everything into consideration, how likely is it that you will make a genuine effort to find a new job within the next year?	1 = very likely 2 = somewhat likely 3 = not at all likely
Job Clout	a. How much does your job allow you to make a lot of decisions on your own? b. How much say do you have over what happens on your job?	2 = no clout 8 = high clout (Items a-b: 1 = not at all; none 2 = a little 3 = somewhat; some 4 = a lot)
Job Performance	How good would you say you are at doing this kind of work?	1 = not very good 2 = just average 3 = a little better than average 4 = very good

133

VARIABLES	ITEMS	RESPONSE CODES
WORK (continued)		
Talking with Others	Please tell me how true each is of your job: I am given a lot of chances to talk with the people I work with.	1 = not at all true 2 = not very true 3 = somewhat true 4 = very true
Achievement Motive at Work[1]	a. What kind of job would you want the most – 1) a job where you had to think for yourself	2 = low achievement motive 5 = high achievement motive
Affiliation Motive at Work[1]	2) a job where the people you work with are a nice group	2 = low affiliation motive 5 = high affiliation motive
Power Motive at Work[1]	3) a job where you have a lot to say in what's going on b. Which of these three would you want the least?	2 = low power motive 5 = high power motive
III. FAMILY (Chapter Five):		
Parental Adequacy	Many men feel that they're not as good fathers as they would like to be. Have you ever felt this way?	1 = yes 2 = no
Marital Happiness	Taking all things together, how would you describe your marriage –– would you say your marriage was very happy, a little happier than average, just about average, or not too happy?	1 = not too happy 2 = just about average 3 = little happier than average 4 = very happy

134

VARIABLES	ITEMS	RESPONSE CODES
FAMILY (continued)		
Marriage Problems	Even in cases where married people are happy there have often been times in the past when they weren't too happy-- when they had problems getting along with each other. Has this ever been true for you?	1 = yes 2 = no
Adequacy as Husband	Many men feel that they're not as good husbands as they would like to be. Have you ever felt this way?	1 = yes 2 = no
Getting Most From Marriage	All in all, who would you say gets more out of being married - you, your wife, or both about equal?	1 = self 2 = about equal 3 = wife
IV. SOCIAL RELATIONSHIPS (Chapter Six):		
Neighbors Known	About how many of your neighbors do you know well enough to visit or call on? Would you say you have many, several, a few, or none?	1 = none 2 = a few 3 = several 4 = many
Neighbors Visited	About how often do you visit with any of your neighbors, either at their homes or at your own? Would you say more than once a week, once a week, a few times a month, once a month, or less than once a month?	1 = less than once a month 2 = once a month 3 = a few times a month 4 = once a week 5 = more than once a week

[1] Derivation of the job motive variables' code structure is given in the first section of Chapter Four, under the subhead, "Motives at Work."

VARIABLES	ITEMS	RESPONSE CODES
SOCIAL RELATIONSHIPS (continued)		
Visits with Friends/Relatives	About how often do you get together with friends or relatives-- I mean things like going out together or visiting in each other's homes. Would you say more than once a week, once a week, a few times a month, once a month, or less than once a month?	1 = never 2 = less than once a month 3 = once a month 4 = few times a month 5 = once a week 6 = more than once a week
Friends/Relatives Free to Talk With	Now, think of the friends and relatives you feel free to talk with about your worries and problems or can count on for advice or help-- would you say you have many, several, a few, or no such friends or relatives?	1 = none 2 = a few 3 = several 4 = many
Talking With Friends/Relatives	How often, if ever, have you talked with friends or relatives about your problems when you were worried, or asked them for advice or help-- very often, often, sometimes, rarely, or never?	1 = never 2 = rarely 3 = sometimes 4 = often 5 = very often
Satisfaction With Friends	Do you feel you have as many friends as you want, or would you like to have more friends?	1 = as many friends as wants 2 = would like more friends

VARIABLES	ITEMS	RESPONSE CODES

SOCIAL RELATIONSHIPS
(continued)

Social Connectedness

I have some statements here that describe the way some people are and feel. I'll read them one at a time and you just tell me how true they are for you—whether they're very true for you, pretty true, not very true, or not true at all.

a. No one cares much what happens to me.

b. I often wish that people would listen to me more.

c. I often wish that people liked me more than they do.

d. These days I really don't know who I can count on for help.

4 = low connectedness
16 = high connectedness

(Items a-d:
1 = very true
2 = pretty true
3 = not very true
4 = not true at all

137

APPENDIX B†

PERCENTAGES WITHIN AGE GROUPS OF FIRST AND SECOND MOST IMPORTANT VALUES

Table B1 Percentages within Age Groups of First Most Important Value*

Age	Belonging	Excitement	Warm Relations	Self-Fulfillment	Respect from Others	Fun and Enjoyment	Security	Self-Respect	Accomplishment	Total
25-29	1.3%	0%	11.7%	18.2%	6.5%	13.0%	32.5%	7.8%	9.1%	100%
30-34	8.0%	0%	13.3%	5.3%	8.0%	5.3%	21.3%	20.0%	18.7%	100%
35-39	6.6%	0%	13.2%	5.3%	3.9%	11.8%	18.4%	19.7%	21.1%	100%
40-44	1.5%	0%	4.6%	6.2%	9.2%	6.2%	24.6%	26.2%	21.5%	100%
45-49	6.3%	0%	12.7%	7.9%	4.8%	3.2%	17.5%	33.3%	14.3%	100%
50-54	5.6%	0%	8.3%	13.9%	8.3%	2.8%	11.1%	30.6%	19.4%	100%
55-59	16.4%	0%	7.5%	4.5%	13.4%	0%	19.4%	28.4%	10.4%	100%
60-64	5.8%	1.9%	19.2%	3.8%	7.7%	0%	21.2%	28.8%	11.5%	100%
65-69	8.8%	0%	17.6%	0%	14.7%	5.9%	26.5%	20.6%	5.9%	100%

* χ^2 (64) = 111.04, p = .0002.

† Rows may not add up to exactly 100% (being off by one or two tenths—e.g. 99.9% or 100.1%) due to the rounding out of numbers within the computer program. This is true for Tables B1 through B6.

Table B2 Percentages within Age Groups of First Most Important Value for Non-College-Educated Men*

Age	Belonging	Excitement	Warm Relations	Self-Fulfillment	Respect from Others	Fun and Enjoyment	Security	Self-Respect	Accomplishment	Total
25-29	2.3%	0%	6.8%	18.2%	6.8%	13.6%	34.1%	6.8%	11.4%	100%
30-34	12.2%	0%	14.6%	2.4%	14.6%	9.8%	19.5%	12.2%	14.6%	100%
35-39	11.6%	0%	18.6%	7.0%	4.7%	9.3%	14.0%	14.0%	20.9%	100%
40-44	3.0%	0%	3.0%	6.1%	18.2%	6.1%	24.2%	21.2%	18.2%	100%
45-49	10.3%	0%	15.4%	7.7%	7.7%	0%	23.1%	25.6%	10.3%	100%
50-54	9.5%	0%	4.8%	9.5%	14.3%	4.8%	9.5%	38.1%	9.5%	100%
55-59	19.0%	0%	4.8%	2.4%	16.7%	0%	23.8%	28.6%	4.8%	100%
60-64	4.4%	2.2%	17.8%	4.4%	8.9%	0%	24.4%	24.4%	13.3%	100%
65-69	11.1%	0%	18.5%	0%	18.5%	7.4%	22.2%	14.8%	7.4%	100%

*χ^2 (64) = 86.872, p = .0302.

Table B3 Percentages within Age Groups of First Most Important Value for College-Educated Men*

Age	Belonging	Excitement	Warm Relations	Self-Fulfillment	Respect from Others	Fun and Enjoyment	Security	Self-Respect	Accomplishment	Total
25-29	0%	0%	18.2%	18.2%	6.1%	12.1%	30.3%	9.1%	6.1%	100%
30-34	2.9%	0%	11.8%	8.8%	0%	0%	23.5%	29.4%	23.5%	100%
35-39	0%	0%	6.1%	3.0%	3.0%	15.2%	24.2%	27.3%	21.2%	100%
40-44	0%	0%	6.3%	6.3%	0%	6.3%	25.0%	31.3%	25.0%	100%
45-49	0%	0%	8.3%	8.3%	0%	8.3%	8.3%	45.8%	20.8%	100%
50-54	0%	0%	13.3%	20.0%	0%		13.3%	20.0%	33.3%	100%
55-59	12.0%	0%	12.0%	8.0%	8.0%	0%	12.0%	28.0%	20.0%	100%
60-64	14.3%	0%	28.6%	0%	0%	0%	0%	57.1%	0%	100%
65-69	0%	0%	14.3%	0%	0%	0%	42.9%	42.9%	0%	100%

*χ^2 (56) = 76.508, p = .0357.

Table B4 Percentages within Age Groups of Second Most Important Value*

Age	Belonging	Excitement	Warm Relations	Self-Fulfillment	Respect from Others	Fun and Enjoyment	Security	Self-Respect	Accomplishment	Total
25-29	3.9%	3.9%	14.3%	13.0%	5.2%	24.7%	14.3%	5.2%	15.6%	100%
30-34	12.0%	0%	8.0%	20.0%	10.7%	9.3%	10.7%	5.3%	24.0%	100%
35-39	2.7%	1.3%	10.7%	9.3%	5.3%	14.7%	20.0%	5.3%	30.7%	100%
40-44	10.8%	0%	16.9%	6.2%	7.7%	4.6%	24.6%	6.2%	23.1%	100%
45-49	9.5%	3.2%	19.0%	15.9%	9.5%	6.3%	11.1%	7.9%	17.5%	100%
50-54	11.1%	0%	16.7%	8.3%	11.1%	11.1%	16.7%	2.8%	22.2%	100%
55-59	10.4%	0%	16.4%	11.9%	16.4%	6.0%	13.4%	4.5%	20.9%	100%
60-64	2.0%	0%	9.8%	2.0%	9.8%	9.8%	25.5%	15.7%	25.5%	100%
65-69	8.8%	0%	26.5%	2.9%	14.7%	8.8%	2.9%	17.6%	17.6%	100%

*χ^2 (64) = 103.99, p = .0012.

141

Table B5 Percentages within Age Groups of Second Most Important Value for Non-College-Educated Men*

Age	Belonging	Excitement	Warm Relations	Self-Fulfillment	Respect from Others	Fun and Enjoyment	Security	Self-Respect	Accomplishment	Total
25-29	4.5%	6.8%	18.2%	9.1%	2.3%	22.7%	18.2%	4.5%	13.6%	100%
30-34	17.1%	0%	9.8%	7.3%	12.2%	9.8%	12.2%	7.3%	24.4%	100%
35-39	4.8%	2.4%	14.3%	7.1%	9.5%	19.0%	19.0%	4.8%	19.0%	100%
40-44	9.1%	0%	27.3%	3.0%	3.0%	9.1%	27.3%	3.0%	18.2%	100%
45-49	12.8%	2.6%	17.9%	7.7%	15.4%	7.7%	15.4%	10.3%	10.3%	100%
50-54	9.5%	0%	19.0%	4.8%	9.5%	9.5%	23.8%	0%	23.8%	100%
55-59	9.5%	0%	14.3%	9.5%	23.8%	9.5%	14.3%	4.8%	14.3%	100%
60-64	2.3%	0%	11.4%	2.3%	11.4%	11.4%	20.5%	18.2%	22.7%	100%
65-69	7.4%	0%	33.3%	3.7%	18.5%	7.4%	3.7%	18.5%	7.4%	100%

*χ^2 (64) = 78.633, p = .1031 (n.s.).

Table B6 Percentages within Age Groups of Second Most Important Value for College-Educated Men*

Age	Belonging	Excitement	Warm Relations	Self-Fulfillment	Respect from Others	Fun and Enjoyment	Security	Self-Respect	Accomplishment	Total
25-29	3.0%	0%	9.1%	18.2%	9.1%	27.3%	9.1%	6.1%	18.2%	100%
30-34	5.9%	0%	5.9%	35.3%	8.8%	8.8%	8.8%	2.9%	23.5%	100%
35-39	0%	0%	6.1%	12.1%	0%	9.1%	21.2%	6.1%	45.5%	100%
40-44	12.5%	0%	6.3%	9.4%	12.5%	0%	21.9%	9.4%	28.1%	100%
45-49	4.2%	4.2%	20.8%	29.2%	0%	4.2%	4.2%	4.2%	29.2%	100%
50-54	13.3%	0%	13.3%	13.3%	13.3%	13.3%	6.7%	6.7%	20.0%	100%
55-59	12.0%	0%	20.0%	16.0%	4.0%	0%	12.0%	4.0%	32.0%	100%
60-64	0%	0%	0%	0%	0%	0%	57.1%	0%	42.9%	100%
65-69	14.3%	0%	0%	0%	0%	14.3%	0%	14.3%	57.1%	100%

*χ^2 (64) = 90.586, p = .0161.

143

References

Allison, P. D. Testing for interaction in multiple regression. *American Journal of Sociology*, 1977, *83*, 144–153.

Andrews, F. M., & Withey, S. B. *Social Indicators of Well Being*. New York: Plenum Press, 1976.

Axelson, L. J. Personal adjustment in the postparental period. *Marriage and Family Living*, 1960, *22*, 66–68.

Babbie, E. R. *Survey Research Methods*. Belmont, Calif.: Wadsworth, 1973.

Back, K. W., & Bourque, L. B. Life graphs: Aging and cohort effect. *Journal of Gerontology*, 1970, *25*, 249–255.

Baltes, P. B. Longitudinal and cross-sectional sequences in the study of age and generation effects. *Human Development*, 1968, *11*, 145–171.

Bardwick, J. M. Middle age and a sense of future. *Merrill-Palmer Quarterly*, 1978, *24*, 129–138.

Bernstein, B. Social class, language and socialization. In B. Bernstein, ed., *Class Codes and Control, Vol. 1: Theoretical Studies Towards a Sociology of Language*. London: Routeledge and Kegan Paul, 1970.

Birren, J. E. Toward an experimental psychology of aging. *American Psychologist*, 1970, *25*, 124–135.

Boneau, C. A. The effects of violations of assumptions underlying the *t*-test. *Psychological Bulletin*, 1960, *57*, 49–64.

Borland, D. C. Research on middle age: An assessment. *The Gerontologist*, 1978, *18*, 379–386.

Bourque, L. B., & Back, K. W. The middle years seen through the life graph. *Sociological Symposium*, 1969, *3*, 19–29.

Breytspraak, L. M. Achievement and the self-concept in middle age. In E. Palmore, ed., *Normal Aging II*. Durham, N.C.: Duke University Press, 1974.

Brim, O. G. Theories of the male mid-life crisis. *The Counseling Psychologist*, 1976, *6*, 2–9.

Burr, W. R. Satisfaction with various aspects of marriage over the life cycle: A random middle-class sample. *Journal of Marriage and the Family*, 1970, *32*, 29–37.

Cameron, P. The generation gap: Which generation is believed powerful versus generational members' self-appraisals of power. *Developmental Psychology*, 1970, *3*, 403–404.

Campbell, A.; Converse, P. E; & Rodgers, W. L. *The Quality of American Life*. New York: Russell Sage, 1976.

Chilman, C. S. Families in development at mid-stage of the family life cycle. *The Family Coordinator*, 1968, *17*, 297–312.

Clausen, J. A. The life course of individuals. In M. W. Riley, M. Johnson, & A. Foner, eds., *Aging and Society*, vol. III. New York: Russell Sage, 1972.

Clausen, J. A. Glimpses into the social world of middle age. *International Journal of Aging and Human Development*, 1976, *7*, 99–106.

Cronbach, L. Coefficient alpha and the internal structure of tests. *Psychometrika*, 1951, *16*, 297–334.

Cutler, N. E. Age variations in the dimensionality of life satisfaction. *Journal of Gerontology*, 1979, *34*, 573–578.

Deutscher, I. The quality of postparental life. In B. L. Neugarten, ed., *Middle Age and Aging*. Chicago: University of Chicago Press, 1968.

Deutscher, I. From parental to post-parental life: Exploring shifting expectations. *Sociological Symposium*, 1969, *3*, 47–60.

Douvan, E.; Veroff, J.; & Kulka, R. *A Study of Modern Living*. Ann Arbor, Mich.: Institute for Social Research, University of Michigan, 1976.

Drevenstedt, J. Perceptions of onsets of young adulthood, middle age, and old age. *Journal of Gerontology*, 1976, *31*, 53–57.

Elder, G. H. Family history and the life course. *Journal of Family History*, 1977, *2*, 279–304.

Elder, G. H., & Rockwell, R. C. Economic depression and postwar opportunity in men's lives: A study of life patterns and health. In R. G. Simmons, ed., *Research in Community and Mental Health: An Annual Compilation of Research*. Greenwich, Conn.: JAI Press, 1978.

Erikson, E. H. *Childhood and Society*. New York: Norton, 1950.

Erikson, E. H. Adulthood and world views. Unpublished paper prepared for Conference on Love and Work in Adulthood, American Academy of Arts and Sciences, Palo Alto, Calif., May, 1977.

Fiske, M. Changing hierarchies of commitment in adulthood. Unpublished paper prepared for Conference on Love and Work in Adulthood, American Academy of Arts and Sciences, Palo Alto, Calif., May, 1977.

Frenkel-Brunswik, E. Adjustments and reorientation in the course of the life span. In. B. L. Neugarten, ed., *Middle Age and Aging*. Chicago: University of Chicago Press, 1968.

Fried, B. *The Middle Age Crisis*. New York: Harper & Row, 1976.

Glenn, N. D. Psychological well being in the post-parental stages: Some evidence from national surveys. *Journal of Marriage and the Family*, 1975, *37*, 105–110.

Glenn, N. D. *Cohort Analysis.* Beverly Hills, Calif.: Sage Publications, 1977.

Glick, P. C. Updating the life cycle of the family. *Journal of Marriage and the Family,* 1977, *39,* 5–13.

Gould, R. L. The phases of adult life: A study in developmental psychology. *American Journal of Psychiatry,* 1972, *129,* 521–531.

Gould, R. L. *Transformations.* New York: Simon & Schuster, 1978.

Gurin, G.; Veroff, J.; & Feld, S. *Americans View Their Mental Health.* New York: Basic Books, 1960.

Hays, W. L. *Statistics for the Social Sciences.* New York: Holt, Rinehart, & Winston, 1973.

Hess, B. Friendship. In M. W. Riley, M. Johnson, & A. Foner, eds., *Aging and Society,* vol. III. New York: Russell Sage, 1972.

Horrocks, J. E., & Mussman, M. C. Middlescence: Age related stress periods during adult years. *Genetic Psychology Monographs,* 1970, *82,* 119–159.

Hyde, J. S., & Phillis, D. E. Androgeny across the life span. *Developmental Psychology,* 1979, *15,* 334–336.

Jackson, D. W. Advanced aged adults' reflections of middle age. *The Gerontologist,* 1974, *14,* 255–257.

Jaffe, A. J. The middle years: Neither too young nor too old. Special issue of *Industrial Gerontology.* Washington, D.C.: National Council on the Aging, 1971.

Jaques, E. Death and the mid-life crisis. *International Journal of Psychoanalysis,* 1965, *46,* 502–514.

Jung, C. G. *Modern Man in Search of a Soul.* New York: Harcourt Brace Jovanovich, 1933, ch. 5, The stages of life, pp. 95–114.

Kahle, L. R.; Kulka, R. A.; & Klingel, D. M. Low adolescent self-esteem leads to multiple interpersonal problems: A test of social adaptation theory. *Journal of Personality and Social Psychology,* in press.

Kerckhoff, R. K. Marriage and middle age. *The Family Coordinator,* 1976, *25,* 5–11.

Kerlinger, F. N. *Foundations of Behavioral Research.* New York: Holt, Rinehart & Winston, 1967.

Kish, L., & Hess, I. The survey research center's national sample of dwellings. Ann Arbor, Mich.: Institute for Social Research, The University of Michigan, 1965.

Klingel, D., & Kulka, R. Comparison between modern living respondent characteristics and 1970/1976 Bureau of Census figures for the United States population. Project Memo, Institute for Social Research, The University of Michigan, Ann Arbor, March 1978.

Kulka, R. A.; Veroff, J.; Douvan, E. Social class and the use of professional help for personal problems: 1957 and 1976. *Journal of Health and Social Behavior,* 1979, *20,* 2–17.

Labovitz, S. Some observations on measurement and statistics. *Social Forces,* 1967, *46,* 151–160.

Labovitz, S. The assignment of numbers to rank order categories. *American Sociological Review,* 1970, *35,* 515–524.

LeShan, E. *The Wonderful Crisis of Middle Age.* New York: Warner Books, 1973.

Levinson, D. J. *The Seasons of a Man's Life.* New York: Alfred A. Knopf, 1978.

Lindquist, E. F. *Design and Analysis of Experiments in Psychology and Education.* Boston: Houghton Mifflin, 1953.

Locksley, A. The effects of occupational experiences on marital attitudes and behavior.

Unpublished doctoral dissertation, University of Michigan, Ann Arbor, 1978.

Lowenthal, M. F., & Chiriboga, D. Transition to the empty nest. *Archives of General Psychiatry*, 1972, *26*, 8–14.

Lowenthal, M. F., & Chiriboga, D. Social stress and adaptation: Toward a life course perspective. In C. Eisdorfer & M. P. Lawton, eds., *The Psychology of Adult Development and Aging*. Washington, D.C.: American Psychological Association, 1973.

Lowenthal, M. F., & Robinson, B. Social networks and isolation. In R. H. Binstock & E. Shanas, eds., *Handbook of Aging and the Social Sciences*. New York: Van Nostrand Reinhold, 1976.

Lowenthal, M. F., & Weiss, L. Intimacy and crises in adulthood. *The Counseling Psychologist*, 1976, *6*, 10–15.

Lowenthal, M. F.; Thurnher, M.; Chiriboga, D.; et al. *Four Stages of Life*. San Francisco: Jossey Bass, 1975.

Maas, H. S., & Kuypers, J. A. *From 30 to 70*. San Francisco: Jossey Bass, 1974.

Mancini, J. A. Sex differences and domains of life satisfaction among middle aged adults. Unpublished paper presented at the annual meeting of the Gerontological Society, Dallas, November 1978.

Mayer, N. *The Male Mid-Life Crisis: Fresh Starts after 40*. New York: Doubleday, 1978.

Mayer, T. F. Middle age and occupational processes: An empirical essay. *Sociological Symposium*, 1969, *3*, 89–106.

Meile, R. L. Age and sex differences in psychiatric treatment. *Sociological Symposium*, 1969, *3*, 107–113.

Neter, J., & Wasserman, W. *Applied Linear Statistical Models*. Homewood, Illinois: Richard D. Irwin, 1974.

Neugarten, B. L. Adult personality: Toward a psychology of the life cycle. In B. L. Neugarten, ed., *Middle Age and Aging*. Chicago: University of Chicago Press, 1968a.

Neugarten, B. L. The awareness of middle age. In B. L. Neugarten, ed., *Middle Age and Aging*. Chicago: University of Chicago Press, 1968b.

Neugarten, B. L. Personality change in late life: A developmental perspective. In C. Eisdorfer & M. P. Lawton, eds., *The Psychology of Adult Development and Aging*. Washington, D.C.: American Psychological Association, 1973.

Neugarten, B. L. Adaptation and the life cycle. *The Counseling Psychologist*, 1976, *6*, 16–20.

Neugarten, B. L., & Datan, N. The middle years. In S. Arieti, ed., *American Handbook of Psychiatry*. New York: Basic Books, 1974.

Neugarten, B. L., & Gutman, D. L. Age–sex roles and personality in middle age: A thematic apperception study. In B. L. Neugarten, ed., *Middle Age and Aging*. Chicago: University of Chicago Press, 1968.

Nunnally, J. *Psychometric Theory*. New York: McGraw-Hill, 1967.

Pearlin, L. I., & Johnson, J. S. Marital status, life strains and depression. *American Sociological Review*, 1977, *42*, 704–715.

Riegel, K. F. Time and change in the development of the individual and society. In H. W. Reese, ed., *Advances in Child Development and Behavior*, vol. 7. New York: Academic Press, 1972.

Riegel, K. F. Dialectic operations: The final period of cognitive development. *Human*

Development, 1973, *16,* 346–370.

Riegel, K. F. Adult life crises: A dialectic interpretation of development. In N. Datan & L. H. Ginsberg, eds., *Life Span Developmental Psychology: Normative Life Crises.* New York: Academic Press, 1975.

Rogers, K. Crisis at the mid-point of life. *New Society,* 1974, 15, 413–415.

Rokeach, M. *The Nature of Human Values.* New York: Free Press, 1973.

Rollins, B. C., & Cannon, K. L. Marital satisfaction over the family life cycle: A reevaluation. *Journal of Marriage and the Family,* 1974, *36,* 271–282.

Rollins, B. C., & Feldman, H. Marital satisfaction over the family life cycle. *Journal of Marriage and the Family,* 1970, *32,* 20–28.

Rosenberg, M. *Society and the Adolescent Self Image.* Princeton, N.J.: Princeton University Press, 1965.

Rosenberg, S. D., & Farrell, M. P. Identity and crisis in middle aged men. *International Journal of Aging and Human Development,* 1976, 7, 153–170.

Rosow, I. *Social Integration and the Aged,* New York: Free Press, 1967.

Rubin, L. B. *Worlds of Pain.* New York: Basic Books, 1976.

Rubin, L. B. *Women of a Certain Age: The Midlife Search for Self.* New York: Harper & Row, 1979.

Schaie, K. W. A general model for the study of developmental problems. *Psychological Bulletin,* 1965, *64,* 92–107.

Schaie, K. W. Toward a stage theory of adult cognitive development. *International Journal of Aging and Human Development,* 1977–1978, *8,* 129–138.

Serlin, E. R. Emptying the nest: Is the launching stage a developmental crisis in the family life cycle? Unpublished doctoral dissertation, University of Michigan, Ann Arbor, Department of Psychology, 1979.

Shanan, J., & Sharon, M. Personality and cognitive functioning of Israeli males during the middle years. *Human Development,* 1965, *8,* 2–15.

Sheehy, G. *Passages.* New York: E. P. Dutton, 1974.

Soddy, K. *Men in Middle Life.* London: J. B. Lippincott, Co., 1967.

Thurnher, M. Goals, values, and life evaluations at the preretirement stage. *Journal of Gerontology,* 1974, *29,* 85–96.

Thurnher, M. Midlife marriage: Sex differences in evaluation and perspectives. *International Journal of Aging and Human Development,* 1976, 7, 129–135.

Vaillant, G. E. *Adaptation to Life.* Boston: Little, Brown, 1977.

Veroff, J., & Feld, S. *Marriage and Work in America.* New York: Van Nostrand Reinhold, 1970.

Veroff, J., & Veroff, J. B. Theoretical notes on power motivation. *Merrill-Palmer Quarterly,* 1971, *17,* 59–69.

Veroff, J.; Douvan, E.; & Kulka, R. *Americans View Their Mental Health: 1957–1976.* New York: Basic Books, in press.

Veroff, J.; Feld, S.; & Gurin, G. Dimensions of subjective adjustment. *Journal of Abnormal and Social Psychology,* 1962, *64,* 192–205.

Wilensky, H. L. Orderly careers and social participation: The impact of work history of social integration in the middle mass. In B. L. Neugarten, ed., *Middle Age and Aging.* Chicago: University of Chicago Press, 1968.

Zung, W. A self rating depression scale. *Archives of General Psychiatry,* 1965, *12,* 63–70.

Index

Accomplishment, sense of, *see* Value orientation

Alcoholism, *see* Drinking problems

Analysis of variance (ANOVA), 29–30, 30–31, 32, 36. *See also* Methodology
and family life measures, 97–98, 98–99
and quality of life experience measures, 42–43, 46–49, 53
and social relationships measures, 108–109
and work measures, 80

College-educated men, in education control, 25–27

Contingency tables, 31–32, 36. *See also* Methodology

Contradictions, resolving personal, 9–10

Correlational analysis, 32–33. *See also* Methodology

Correlations, formula comparing, 33–34

Drinking problems measures, 40, 46–52, 64–67. *See also* Well-being

Education control, in method of study, 25–27

Empty-nest syndrome, 15–16. *See also* Family and middle age

Family and middle age, 121–122
age differences (results), 97–100
age interactions between family and well-being (results), 102–104
age interactions in measures of family life (results), 100–102
empty-nest syndrome, 15–16
marriage, middle-aged, 17–19
measures of family life, 96–97
methodology of study, 24–25
parenthood, problems of, 16–17
results, summary of, 104–105

Friendships, 19–20, 107, 108–109. *See also* Social relationships and middle age

Generativity, middle age and, 10–11

Group Effect Decomposition Method, 30

Happiness measures, 38, 42–46. *See also* Well-being

Health
middle age and, 7–8
physical ill health, 40–41, 46–52

Illness, physical, 40–41, 46–52

Immobilization, psychological, 39–40, 46–52, 113

Indices, construction of, 28. *See also* Methodology

Interactions, detection of, 32–35. *See also* Methodology

Internal psychological state measures, 38–39, 42–46. *See also* Well-being

Job clout, 70, 75–77, 83, 87–88, 94–95. *See also* Work and middle age

Job performance, 71, 77–78

Job relations, 71, 79–80, 83–87

Job satisfaction, 70, 72–73, 87–88, 94–95

Life satisfaction
measures of, 38, 42–46
sources of, 41, 52–58
work and, 91–93

Marriage, 17–19, 97, 98–100, 100–102, 104–105. *See also* Family and middle age; Life satisfaction
methodology of study, 24–25

Men versus women, in middle age, 3–4

Methodology, 20–21
analysis strategy, 27–35
detection of interactions, 32–35
education control, 25–27
exploratory method, 118–119
indices, construction of, 28
the interview, 22–23
men in families, 24–25
parametric statistics, 29–32
results, structure of, 35–36
sampling design, 23–24
study sample, 24–27

Middle age
alterations at, 7–11
benefits of, 11–12
as crisis, 4–5
defined, 2
family and, *see* Family and middle age
generativity and, 10–11
health and, 7–8, 40–41, 46–52
method of study, *see* Methodology
mortality and, 8
problems, concrete and covert, 5–7
quality of life and, *see* Quality of life experience and middle age
resolving personal contradictions and, 9–10
self-assessment and, 8–9
social relationships and, *see* Social relationships and middle age
work and, *see* Work and middle age

Middle-aged marriage, *see* Marriage

Middle-aged men
  defining, 2
  method of study of, *see* Methodology
  versus middle-aged women, 3–4
  as special population, 1–4
  the total picture, 117–126
  the transition, 2–3, 122–123
Midlife crisis, 2–3, 4–5
Mortality, middle age and, 8

National Institute of Mental Health, 23
Neighbors, 106–107, 108. *See also* Social
  relationships and middle age
Noncollege men, in education control, 25–27

Parametric statistics, 29–32. *See also* Methodology
Parenthood, 96–97, 97–98, 100–102, 104–
  105. *See also* Family and middle age;
  Life satisfaction
  problems of, 16–17
Physical-ill-health measures, 40–41, 46–52
Psychological anxiety measures, 40, 46–52,
  64. *See also* Well-being
Psychological immobilization. *See also* Well-
  being
  measures of, 39–40, 46–52
  social supports and, 113

Quality of life experience and middle age,
  4–12
  age differences in (results), 42–64
  age interactions in measures of well-being,
    (results), 64–67
  defined, 37
  measures of, 37–42
  results, summary of, 67–68
  time orientation, 41–42, 58–61
  value orientation, 42, 61–64
  well-being, 38–41, 42–58

Regression, as an interaction detector, 34–35
Relatives, 107, 108–109. *See also* Family and
  middle age; Social relationships and
  middle age
Research, future of, 124–125. *See also* Methodology

Security, *see* Value orientation
Self-assessment, middle age and, 8–9
Self-esteem
  measures of, 38–39, 42–46
  work and, 90–91
Self-fulfillment, *see* Value orientation
Sex-role crossover, 10
Social class, education and, 25–27
Social connectedness, 107–108, 109, 110–113

Social relationships and middle age, 19–20,
  121–122. *See also* Value orientation
  age differences (results), 108–109
  age interactions between well-being and
    social relationships (results), 110–113
  age interactions in measures of (results),
    110
  friends and relatives, 19, 107, 108–109
  individual differences, 20
  measures of, 106–108
  neighbors, 106–107, 108
  results, summary of, 114–116
  social connectedness, 107–108, 109, 110–
    113
Study of Modern Living, 22–23, 23–24, 25, 28
Survey Research Center, University of Michigan Institute for Social Research, 23

Time orientation, 41–42, 58–61, 68
Time series plots, 31, 36. *See also* Method-
  ology
Transition to middle age, 2–3, 122–123

Value orientation, 42, 61–64, 68

Well-being, 119–120. *See also* Quality of life
  experience and middle age
  age interactions in measures of (results),
    64–67
  and family, age interactions between (re-
    sults), 102–104
  internal psychological state, 38–39, 42–46
  and social relationships, 110–113
  sources of life satisfaction and, 41, 52–58
  symptoms, 39–41, 46–52
  and work, 90–93
Women versus men, in middle age, 3–4
Work and middle age, 120–121. *See also*
  Life satisfaction
  age differences (results), 72–82
  age interactions between work and well-
    being (results), 90–93
  age interactions in measures of work (re-
    sults), 82–90
  deemphasis of work, 13–14
  measures of work, 69–72
  motives at work, 71, 80
  options at work, 13–15
  peak, 12–13
  reemphasis on work, 14
  results, summary of, 93–95
  social scene at work, 14–15
Work commitment, 70, 73–75, 94–95

Zest
  measures of, 38, 42–46
  and work, 93
Zung Depression Scale, 38

Date Due

MAR 21 '88			
MAR 13 '89			